52.2

WOMEN and
SOCIAL CLASS

WOMEN and SOCIAL CLASS

Pamela Abbott and
Roger Sapsford

TAVISTOCK PUBLICATIONS
London and New York

First published in 1987 by
Tavistock Publications Ltd
11 New Fetter Lane, London EC4P 4EE

Published in the USA by
Tavistock Publications
in association with Methuen, Inc.
29 West 35th Street, New York NY 10001

Printed and bound in
Great Britain by Biddles Ltd,
Guildford and Kings Lynn

British Library Cataloguing in Publication Data

Abbott, Pamela
  Women and social class.
  1. Social classes   2. Women – Social
  conditions
  I. Title   II. Sapsford, R.J.
  305.5   HT609

ISBN   0-422-61000-3

Library of Congress Cataloging-in-Publication Data

Abbott, Pamela.
  Women and social class.

  Bibliography: p.
  Includes indexes.
  1. Women – Social conditions.   2. Social classes.
  3. Feminism.   I. Sapsford, Roger.   II. Title.
  HQ1154.A226   1987   305.4'2   87-10211

ISBN   0-422-61000-3 (pbk.)

Contents

Preface

In one sense this is intended not as a 'feminist book' but as a contribution to the mainstream of sociological debate. We cover the topics that one would expect to find in any book on social class: social mobility and the degree to which we live in an 'open' society; determinants or correlates of subjective social class; views on what characteristics are important in assigning class labels; and social imagery, the 'world view' people have of their social environment. The main points are made in part by reference to summaries of the research literature that one would expect to find in such a book. The main difference is that the new data we have to offer are data on women.

In another sense, however, our endeavour is a distinctly feminist one. This is a book about *women* and social class. It starts from the position that it is necessary to incorporate women in social class analysis for both theoretical and empirical reasons. A theory that cannot explain the subordinate position of women is inadequate, and empirical research based on male-only samples cannot adequately reflect the full range of class stratification, social mobility and class awareness, consciousness and action. However, this endeavour has not been without its problems, not least because of the inadequacies of existing theories and concepts. Thus, as Johnstone and Rattanis (1981) have pointed out in reviewing the Oxford Mobility Study,

'It is . . . not at all surprising that there is no recognition here that the 'invisible woman' in the sociology of class is not *simply* the product of women's social subordination to men, but is inscribed in the very structure of discourse for which the occupational order and the market are the central conceptual means for theorising the economy and its relation to class.'   (p. 206)

While we feel that we have demonstrated in this book the need to incorporate women in class analysis, we recognize that how this is to be done is an issue that still requires considerable development of theory and research. We do not claim even to have begun to demonstrate ways in which the incorporation of women could satisfactorily be brought about.

This book, then, is a contribution to the debate on women and class and is one that looks at the issues from the standpoint of women. In this sense it can be seen as a feminist contribution to the debate. We hold the view that feminist sociology must be about ways of incorporating women into sociology – not just about research on women. As we have demonstrated, trying to incorporate women makes us aware of the inaccuracies, about men as well as women, of the conclusions which have been drawn from male-only samples and of the theory about social class which has been based on them.

We are indebted to the DE304 and DE801 Course Teams at the Open University, who gave us permission to use the survey data on which this book is based. We should also like to thank the Open University students on these courses who collected the data and the people who gave their time as respondents. Finally, we acknowledge the help we have received from the computing centres at the Open University, Cambridge University, and Plymouth Polytechnic.

Pamela Abbott
Plymouth Polytechnic

Roger Sapsford
The Open University

1 Women and social class: An overview

In the last twenty or so years feminists have challenged the nature of conventional sociology, arguing that at best the conventionally used categories of analysis are 'sex-blind' and consequently fail to reveal gender differences and inequalities, and at worst they are plainly sexist and divert attention from important gender-related aspects of social life. An ever-growing feminist sociology has appeared during the same period – that is, sociological work that incorporates women as people in their own right rather than, if at all, as some sort of deviation from the male norm. There is controversy within this new tradition as to whether what is needed is research on women, by women, or rather the construction of a new 'mainstream' in sociology by the development of sociological theory, categorization and analytical tools to take account of women and incorporate them in their own right within the 'problematics' of the discipline. The latter approach would mean not just including women in research samples, but the development of adequate theories and theoretical categories so that gender differences can be researched and explained and cannot be overlooked.

It is evident from the debates which have arisen and from inspection of sociological work undertaken in the past that women have been ignored systematically in many of the key areas of sociological interest; they have been seen as marginal or peripheral to them and therefore excluded. This is nowhere more true than in the area of social stratification and social class theory. Most of the main stratification studies undertaken in Britain or the United States have excluded women from their samples; major theoretical lines of social class analysis have either not considered gender inequalities at all or have argued that women are marginal to class analysis.

The core of the conventional view is that stratification theory is concerned with explaining *class* inequalities – inequalities that arise out of the occupational or economic structure of society. As women, it is argued, are marginal to the occupational structure and as their paid employment is conditioned by their familial responsibilities, their social class position is most realistically determined by the occupation of the 'bread-winner', the (male) head of household. In other words, the conventional view asserts that social class inheres not in individuals but in households. The household is the unit of analysis, and the class position of that unit is determined by the occupation of its head. Indeed, the instructions given to interviewers (see Oakley and Oakley 1979) tend to be such that if an adult male is present in a household it is almost certain that his occupation will determine the coding of the class position of that household. This means in practice that some people (mainly adult males) have a class position determined by their own occupation, while other people (mainly, but not exclusively, married women) have their class position determined by the occupation of someone with whom they live.

It is not just that women are ignored in stratification theory – that women's subordinate position is not seen as part of what the theory needs to explain – or that women are excluded from major surveys; more important still is that many women (the majority) are said to have only a derived class position, determined by the occupational experience of a man with whom they live. This is not just a technical convenience of survey coding; it is a theoretical statement that women's experiences, loyalties, and social action are not their own in the sense that men's are. Along with the equally sexist proposition that women are necessarily dependent on men and that gender inequalities are therefore necessarily and a priori less important than male class differences, this curious assumption underlies much conventional stratification theory. The effect is that such theoretical positions undermine their own arguments by failing to provide a comprehensive account of social experience and by failing to provide adequate empirical grounding. They fail in the former by excluding over half the population from their analysis, and in the latter by effectively miscoding that part of the population when they do include it.

The major feminist objections to conventional class theory were first voiced systematically by Acker (1973), who listed five shortcomings in the conventional approach. These were:

(i) the assumption that the family is the rational unit of analysis, with complete class equivalence within it;
(ii) that the social position of the family is determined by the occupation of the head of household;
(iii) that the male is necessarily the head of household, if such a position has to be distinguished;
(iv) that none the less women somehow determine their own class position when they do not happen to be living with an adult male; and
(v) that the inequalities between men and women are inherent and inevitable.

These points of objection have been taken up and expanded by feminists in both the United States and Great Britain. Not only has a theoretical debate developed, but also empirical research to demonstrate how necessary it is to incorporate women into stratification and class theory. As Dex (1985) has pointed out, it is not particular theories of stratification which are being attacked, but *all* the major theories – the American structural–functionalist tradition and the British neo-Weberian and neo-Marxist traditions alike. The basic arguments against all of these are the same and boil down to the theories' inadequacies in terms of both explaining gender inequalities and incorporating women adequately into the explanation even of class inequalities. Indeed, it could be argued that the failure of sociology to incorporate women into class analysis is bound up with its more general failure to change and develop its concepts as society changes. Giddens (1973) has suggested that the failure of social class analysis to develop in response to social change has resulted in a crisis for social theory, which is confused, ambiguous, and lacking in analytical precision. Yet Giddens himself has none the less remained within the malestream tradition as a class theorist, failing to recognize that changes in women's employment histories and a widespread questioning of the inevitability of the separation of public and private spheres (particularly when they are segregated on gender lines) may require radical rethinking of social stratification theory. One might almost believe, as Dex (1985) suggests, that male sociologists *want* women to remain marginal or invisible.

Two broad 'fronts' may be distinguished within the feminist challenge to class theory, both of which are summarized briefly below: the attempt to revise class theory to make sense of women's class relationships, and the wider attempt to recast stratification theory as a whole so that gender differences and inequalities are properly recognized within it. While sympathizing strongly with the latter endeavour, in this book we have concentrated chiefly on the former. We present data from the Open University's People in Society Survey, a source previously untapped except in two recent papers (Abbott and Sapsford 1986; Abbott 1987), together with a critical survey of the available work on women, men, and class relations, to make a preliminary exploration of women's class images and subjective class position and to illustrate how such an analysis of women's social class could add to our ability to theorize class relations adequately.

Women as a class

The first side of the feminist challenge deals with the question of what stratification theory should be able to explain – its range of convenience. The conventional view is that stratification theory is about class divisions determined by occupation, and that these are an intelligible area of study in their own right. Feminists have argued that stratification theory should be equally (or more) concerned with gender inequalities. (The position could be taken further, to assert that an adequate theoretical position would be able to deal with *all* major sources of inequality – class, gender, race, age, etc. It is argued that a theory which is not able to cope with the articulation of the major sources of social inequality cannot adequately explain inequalities based on only one source, because all sources combine to define social position.

The *radical feminist* position has mainly been developed by the French writer Christine Delphy (see for example, 1977, 1981, 1984). Delphy argues that while sociologists have regarded occupational class inequalities as primary, their own research demonstrates that sexual inequality is primary and more fundamental than occupational inequality. Thus women's oppression cannot be seen as secondary to, and therefore less important than, class oppression. Delphy argues that women (or at least, wives) form a class who are exploited by men (husbands).

> 'While the wage-labourer sells his labour-power, the married woman gives hers away: exclusivity and non-payment are intimately connected. To supply unpaid labour within the framework of a universal and personal relationship (marriage) constructs primarily a relationship of slavery.'
>
> (Delphy 1977: 15)

and

> 'the logical consequence of the non-value of a woman's labour is the hunt for a good marriage. But even though a marriage with a man from a capitalist class can raise a woman's standard of living, it does not make her a member of that class. She herself does not own the means of production. Therefore, her standard of living does not depend on her class relationship to the proletariat, but on her serf relations of production with her husband.'
>
> (p.19)

Because women are opposed as a class to men, are exploited by men and therefore have shared interests in opposition to men, and patriarchal structures are fundamental to our form of social organization, it follows that the main axis of differentiation in our society must be gender.

Walby (1986) is another who argues that housewives and husbands form two separate classes. She argues that housework is a distinctive form of work even though the housewife does not receive payment. Domestic work is productive: the housewife produces the labour power of her husband, herself, and her children. The distinctiveness of domestic labour lies in the relations of production under which it is performed. Wives exchange their labour for their maintenance, and therefore wives as a class are exploited by their husbands, in a patriarchal mode of production. (See also Eichler 1980, for another variant of this kind of account.) Walby and Delphy argue, then, that while housewives may differ in their standard of living because their husbands are in different occupational classes, yet they are also to be seen as all members of the same class because of what they share – exploitation by another class (husbands) in a patriarchal mode of production. Stratification theory, they argue, must explain these inequalities – the dominance of men over women – if it is to be seen as adequate. Indeed, given the fundamental importance of gender-based inequalities, this must be its main task.

In Delphy's more recent analysis, co-authored with Diana Leonard (Delphy and Leonard 1986), these arguments have been further developed. They argue not only that 'class or strati-fication analysis, which forefronts a particular form of inequality, cannot therefore be regarded as adequate representation of society as a whole, or even of social inequalities' (p. 72), but go on to demonstrate that the exclusion of women from class analysis also leads to the

> 'misrepresentation of class life-changes, life-styles, patterns of association and socio-political orientation, which they [class theorists] certainly do care about. It also results in gross mis-representation of the mechanisms (notably the hereditary transmission of status) which account for the perpetuation of, and changes within, classes and between classes over time.'
> (p. 73)

Thus they argue that the inclusion of women as a class enables us to understand how fathers' occupational advantage is in-herited by some of their offspring (mainly sons) when other children (notably daughters) are excluded. It also enables us to recognize the different and antagonistic categories and statuses which exist within classes as conventionally defined.

Walby, while stressing the importance of patriarchy as a mode of production, also recognizes that many women will have an occupational class in their own right: women in paid employ-ment have a class location determined by their market position. This point also seems to be recognized implicitly in Delphy's work. Thus in this line of theory some women (housewives in paid employment) have *two* class positions – one determined by their role as housewives and one by their occupation. (By implication this holds for men in employment as well: if women as a class are exploited by husbands as a class, then some men have a class position defined by their marital status as well as an occupational class.) However, radical feminists generally go beyond immediate personal circumstances to the structural position of the gender as a whole and argue that all women, not just married women, are oppressed by men and that patriarchal relations are dominant (see, for example, Millett 1971). One might argue, for example, that the occupational status (market position) of all women is conditioned by the fact that some women marry and that women as a whole are restricted in their career opportunities, for instance, by attitudes among selectors who are conditioned by an expectation of marriage. Evidence of gross overall patriarchal relations might also come from the extent of labour market segregation by gender – the overall concentration of women or men in different occupations and in different hierarchical positions. MacEwan Scott (1986), as a result of a cross-national study, argues that the market which produces such sexual segregation is not itself sex-neutral but shaped by political and ideological pressures. In all societies women are regarded as forming a special category of labour even when there are no longer differences in supply: 'the "gender-embeddedness" of the division of labour is thus an outcome of the wider structure of gender inequality and of the institutional linkages which shape the division of labour'. Thus even when we consider women's class positions as determined by the labour market we have to take account of patriarchally conditioned inequalities between men and women.

The malestream response to this position has varied. On the one hand, it has been argued that class is the major form of inequality and that women are themselves more divided by class inequalities than the sexes are by gender inequalities; the conclusion is that class is a coherent and important area of study in its own right and that class theory does not need to concern itself with questions of gender (Parkin 1972; Lockwood 1986). Alternatively, it may be argued that gender inequalities can be explained adequately by existing theory. Parkin (1979), for instance, has argued that Weberian theories of social stratification, and specifically the concepts of market position and social closure, give an adequate account of gender inequalities (see also Murphy 1984). Mainstream Marxist writers, similarly, have suggested that Marxist theories give an adequate account of the position of women (e.g. Poulantzas 1975; Wright 1985). Marxists argue that the radical feminist position fails to take account of the specific nature of class inequalities in capitalist society. They argue that in the capitalist mode of production it is the bourgeoisie who exploit the proletariat, and that the subordinate position of women can be wholly explained by their position within the bourgeois nuclear family under the capitalist mode of production. Attempts have indeed been made to develop the theory so that gender inequalities can receive more adequate explanation. None the less, the main Marxist concern remains the explanation of how all workers are exploited in a capitalist society – men, women, black, white – and specific explanations for women's subordination have to be incorporated within that more general frame of analysis.

The main development within mainstream Marxist theory to take account of gender relates very much to women's position within the bourgeois nuclear family. It is based on Engels' argument that women's oppression can be seen to begin with the emergence of private property and hence with capitalist class relations, so that the struggle for a classless society logically subsumes the struggle for women's emancipation. Thus the separation of public and private spheres with the development of industrial capitalism meant that women came increasingly to be economically dependent on men and to serve the needs of capitalism by having and caring for children, thus producing the next generation of workers and reproducing the labour power of their husbands (Zaretsky 1976). Women were therefore increasingly excluded from the labour market and did not produce surplus value; failing to be classifiable as producer or exploiter of surplus value, they thereby failed to have a class position of their own. They did, however, come to form part of the industrial reserve army – a group of potential workers who could easily be called into the labour market at times of economic need and just as easily be pushed out again when no longer required. Thus they provided a buffer against the cyclical nature of capitalist economic development. The main thrust of the Marxist argument, then, is very much that the subordinate position of women can be explained by the means and relationships of production under capitalism.

However, *Marxist feminists* have challenged this conventional

Marxist view, arguing that it is inadequate for the same reasons that the malestream sociological view is inadequate and that we need to incorporate explanations of women's ongoing location in the family as the performers of domestic duties in our theoretical explanations in order to understand fully women's position in the labour market – in other words, that theory must adequately explain the relationship between patriarchy and capitalism. *Socialist feminists* such as Heidi Hartmann (1976) have gone further, arguing that the categories within which Marxists operate are themselves sex-blind, and that patriarchal relationships preceded capitalism and will probably succeed it also. In order to understand the subordination of women in the capitalist mode of production, they argue, it is necessary to *articulate* patriarchal with Marxist explanations – to show how the two kinds of explanation interlock to produce processes not directly predictable within either alone: 'capitalist development creates the places for a hierarchy of workers but traditional Marxist categories cannot tell us who will fill which places. Gender and racial hierarchies determine who fills the empty places' (p. 18). Thus radical feminists have argued that sexual oppression is primary, and economic exploitation secondary, and conventional Marxists have argued the reverse. Marxist feminists and socialist feminists have argued that gender and class inequalities have a mutual influence and cannot be analysed in isolation from each other, although Marxist feminists tend on the whole to give primacy to class.

A further interesting line of thought has been advanced by some Marxist feminists, who suggest that dualism – the separation of patriarchal oppression and class exploitation, and thus the need to articulate them in explanations – is itself a historically conditioned phenomenon, consequent on the separation of production from the rest of life, and specific to capitalist society in its present form. 'In treating patriarchy and capitalism as distinct systems we are reading back into history and into other kinds of societies a state of affairs peculiar to our own' (Smith 1983: 2). Smith argues that the domination of men over women in the direct and personal way found under capitalism is specific to that mode of production. She argues that capitalism created two specific kinds of individual – owners of the means of production and individuals owning labour power that they are forced to sell in order to subsist. Capitalism is accompanied by the development of philosophies stressing equality within a democratic system, but by taking the stand-point of the proletariat it is possible to see that private property is a barrier to equality and democracy. If we go beyond this and take the standpoint of women we can see a further barrier to equality: the inequality that exists in the family between men and women. An analysis of the relation of women's domestic labour to labour power sold as a commodity demonstrates that the individual worker is 'produced' through his wife's domestic labour, and Smith argues that this is as true in the middle class as the proletarian family. She concludes that the separation of consumption from production in the capitalist mode of produc-tion means that the exploitation of women by men in integral to that mode.

Susan Himmelweit (1983) echoes many of these arguments and argues that the problem is not assigning priority of explanation to patriarchy or capitalism as a form of oppression, or favouring one struggle over the other, or even finding some way of integrating them within the body of theory, but recognizing that the problem is a historical and political one and that the solution will also be a political one – the transfor-mation of society by reintegrating production into life itself. This, she suggests, involves more than transforming the means of production or a change from production for profit to produc-tion for use; rather, it involves recognizing that production takes no ultimate priority over the rest of life, that the needs of the family and of personal life are also real needs, and conversely that labour and economic problems are not absent from family life. In immediate practical terms this would mean the provision of shorter and flexible working hours for child-carers, of nur-series, of 'wages for housework', or some such means of assur-ing the financial independence of carers, etc. In the longer term it would mean breaking down the separation by gender of what we currently see as two separate spheres of life, the equal participation (in principle and according to personal needs and desires) of both genders in both parts of life, and thus inevitably the removal of stigma and penalty from one of them.

As can be seen, the debate concerning the incorporation of women into stratification theory is a complex one at this level, and different 'schools' take different lines on how it should be achieved. What all the feminist lines so far discussed have in common, however, is the view that stratification theory must be able to account for gender disparities as well as (or even instead of) class inequalities. The malestream response, shared by what we have labelled 'conventional' Marxists, is either that stratification theory already does this quite adequately or that it is not called upon to do so, being concerned with *class* inequalities and having no need to go beyond the bounds of class in order to forge coherent explanations.

Women in class theory

The second principal challenge brought by feminists against conventional class analysis – the one to which this book is intended as a contribution – concerns the necessity for it to take account of women's class position as well as men's, not only because they are over half the population, but also because by excluding women we in fact come to an inadequate understanding of the class position even of men. We agree with Walby (1986) that feminist stratification theory should 'not confine itself merely to elaborating more accurate rankings of life-style and prestige, which include women as well as men'. None the less, we see the elaboration and rectification of conventional class theory to include women as a relevant activity for sociologists influenced by feminist arguments and research. We would assert the need to incorporate women into class analysis, to close the gap in our knowledge and understanding that exists because their role in the class system and their relation to status hierarchies have been ignored. Thus as Morgan and Taylorson argue:

'Whether we adopt some version of a Marxist or a Weberian analysis, in practice our concern is with occupational groupings – their different relations to the mode of production, their different rankings in term of income, power and prestige, and so on. Since most women have for most of their lives worked and held occupational identities and since most women at some time contribute to the husband's income, women should clearly occupy a place in studies of class and stratification in their own right.'   (1983: 8)

and, as Allen (1982) points out,

This argument changes not only our perception of women's position, but of class relations, introducing specifications and inconsistencies which remain uninvestigated for both men and women.'   (p. 147)

Furthermore, Allen warns us that

'those who endeavour to analyse women's position in the class structure enter a workshop which is lamentably ill-equipped for the task. There are few tools but, more important, little recognition that the task requires even burnished tools, let alone freshly fashioned ones.'   (p. 137)

A number of studies have been carried out which demonstrate that women's class makes a difference to the class of a household (e.g. Heath and Britten 1984; Britten and Heath 1983; Pahl and Wallace 1985) and that incorporating women makes us rethink some of our existing understanding of class (e.g. Chapman 1984; Crompton and Mann 1986; Crompton and Jones 1984). The response of malestream sociology to the feminist challenge that women should be incorporated into social class analysis – that a line of theory which cannot account for the experiences of over half the population cannot be considered adequate – has generally been either a determined defence of the conventional position that women are marginal in this context (Goldthorpe 1983; Lockwood 1986; Giddens 1973) or the assertion that existing theory is adequate to deal with them without much backing for this claim (e.g. Parkin 1979; Murphy 1984). The major recent defence of the conventional view has been offered by Goldthorpe (1983, 1984) and responded to directly by Stanworth (1984), Heath and Britten (1984) and Walby (1986). If we examine this debate in some detail we shall be able to see clearly the main arguments which have been developed in the last twenty years for and against the incorporation of women into class analysis in the narrow sense. (Much of the debate has been engaged in by sociologists who work within a neo-Weberian class framework.)

The main and basic assumption of the malestream position is that a woman's place is in the family and that, apart from the (male) bread-winner's linkage to the economy, the family is outside class analysis. Female employment is seen as subordinate to the housewife role. Rather than taking up the difficult challenge of developing class theory to take account of women's experiences, Goldthorpe (1983) has chosen to restate and defend the conventional view. He argues that the whole point of the conventional view is that it does recognize the subordinate position of women in society generally, by assigning them a subordinate or derivative position with regard to social class. Women's role in the family, he argues, and their social and economic life-chances, including whether taking paid employment is possible for them, are largely determined by the socio-economic position of the family, which in turn is determined by the socio-economic position of its head, the husband. He would also argue that little injustice is done even in the case where the wife does undertake paid employment outside the home, because 'cross-class' marriages with husbands and wives in jobs which fall into different occupational classes are in fact fairly rare. The one common case, of a woman in routine non-manual employment married to a skilled manual worker, he sees as an artefact of the asymmetries of work distribution and therefore not really an exception to this rule. Such families, he would assert, are in essence working class, and routine non-manual labour should be categorized as working-class for women.

Claims such as these have increasingly been challenged by feminists. West (1978), for instance, maintains that even if women are not a class, that does not mean that women do not occupy an independent place in the class structure. She argues that it is necessary to take account of women's labour market position and to recognize that not all women do in fact live with an adult male; inequalities within families also deserve recognition. Furthermore, she argues, women's place in the division of labour is what it is not only because of female domestic labour but also because of how labour is divided outside the home. It is necessary, she suggests, to examine the available places in the division of labour and to look at the places actually occupied by women if we want to understand the place of women in the class structure. This would enable us to understand better the class structure as a whole, the place of women within it, and the role of sexual divisions. She suggests that the combination of female wage labour with domestic work has highly complex consequences for class structure and class consciousness. She argues that the problems posed for class analysis and stratification theory by women's employment are only avoided, not solved, by retreating into the conventional position that the family is the unit of stratification and that a woman's class position is determined by that of her husband.

Similarly, Garnsey (1978) suggests that while the family is a relevant category, taking it as the only unit of analysis obscures the inequalities between women's and men's positions within the family and the different market and work situations which they face outside it. She argues that the dual role of women (or at least, of some women) means that they have a specific labour market position and that the division of labour between men and women within the household also affects how women stand in the market. Women are at the bottom, in employment terms, within each social class, and this consistent inequality needs to be seen as central to the study of stratification because it pervades the whole social structure. The participation of women in the labour market affects the nature of that market for men as well as for women. Women are concentrated in lowly paid, low-status jobs, and this affects the range of jobs available to men. Thus the ways in which female wage labour and domestic labour are combined and interact with each other and with the capitalist system have complex consequences for class structure and class consciousness. Women mostly occupy the buffer zone between the working class and the middle class, a zone which Goldthorpe claims has disappeared (see Chapter 3). Indeed, women form a buffer zone at the bottom of each class.

In her response to Goldthorpe, Stanworth (1984) has argued that to submerge a woman's class position in that of her husband is not justified by the evidence, and that in any case doing so closes off some of the most interesting issues in class analysis. Goldthorpe's approach obscures the extent to which the class experience of wives differs from that of husbands and ignores the extent to which inequalities which divide men and women are themselves an outcome of the class system's operation. Specifically, Stanworth challenges three of Goldthorpe's main arguments: that husbands have a more extensive involvement in the workforce, that wives' patterns of employment can largely be explained by the occupational class position of husbands, and that contemporary marriages are largely homogeneous with respect to class. She demonstrates that none of these three claims carries the implications which Goldthorpe derives from them, and that his own data fail to substantiate the second and third of the claims.

First, Goldthorpe is able to show only that most married women do take time out from the labour market, but other research (e.g. Martin and Roberts 1984) demonstrates that women show a substantial and life-long commitment to paid employment. Furthermore, the pattern is changing, so that the time that women have out of the labour market is tending to decrease. Second, there is little support from Goldthorpe's own data (from the Oxford Mobility Study) for the proposition that a woman's labour market participation is conditioned by her husband's class, and a husband's class seems to have less influence on the timing of a wife's withdrawal from the labour market than her own occupational class does. Third, Stanworth demonstrates that if routine white-blouse workers are re-classified as working class, this does not 'solve' the problem of cross-class marriages. True, the marriage of a manual worker to a routine non-manual woman becomes by fiat no longer cross-class, but at the expense of creating a new large group of cross-class marriages, those involving a routine non-manual woman (now classified as working class) and a *non*-manual man.

The assumption that women acquire derived status from their husbands is similarly under attack. Allen (1982) points out that the wife does not acquire her husband's educational qualifi-cations on marriage, nor does she automatically acquire a socially or politically powerful background as a permanent right. (She often loses them, for instance, on divorce or as a widow.) Nor, presumably, does she lose her own education or her own background if she marries a man less educated or less well-connected than herself. In an attempt to begin to examine how husband's and wife's social class influence each other, Heath (1981; see also Heath and Britten 1984) has looked particularly at cross-class marriages, where the interrelationship should be reasonably apparent. Heath demonstrated that households with a manual husband and a routine non-manual wife are qualitatively and quantitatively different from house-holds without this discordant class membership. Cross-class households have higher incomes than working-class ones; the middle-class wives within them have higher educational qualifications, and so do the working-class men to whom they are married; they have smaller families; and working-class men married to middle-class women are more likely to vote Conservative. Furthermore, when European class theorists have argued that

> '[the] work situation provides the most important set of conditions shaping the social imagery of modern man, for it is at work that relations of superiority and inferiority, of solidarity and separateness, of frustration and achievement are most pervasive, most visible and therefore most influential,'
> (Mackenzie 1975: 173)

it seems odd for someone located within this tradition to try to argue that a woman's social imagery is determined by her *husband's* work experiences rather than her own. It seems likely, surely, that a woman's own work experiences *will* influence her social imagery, and more likely still that her influence on her husband in this respect will be as substantial as his on her. Family situation and relationships in the patriarchal mode of production are likely to have an influence on the social imagery of both husband and wife. (We would accept, however, that the consumption pattern of a household also influences class attitudes, that this is determined by income in large part, and that in our society husbands generally earn more than their wives.)

Finally, Walby (1986) points out a central contradiction in Goldthorpe's position. In the European tradition within which Goldthorpe works there has always been great emphasis on analysing the relationship between class position and political action – defining classes in relationship to each other, as groups of people who have similar socio-economic positions and interests. Indeed, this is what Goldthorpe argues he was doing in constructing the Hope-Goldthorpe Scale (see Chapter 3). The American tradition, conversely, has been to look at class as a continuous prestige ranking. However, if a woman's class position is determined by the occupation of her husband, then effectively class is being determined by standard of living – that is, by consumption patterns rather than by market position – and this is incompatible with any analysis in which class location is defined by the individual's market or work position. Thus while women's class is a ranking, in the American tradition, by husband's occupation, men's is determined by their market location in accordance with the European tradition. Goldthorpe would presumably reply that a wife's interests are those of her family, and derived from her husband's class position, so a wife in a working-class family must share the interests of the working class. Like other writers, however, we fail to see the logical necessity for wives' interests to coincide with those of husbands. They may do so contingently, but empirical research might equally demonstrate cases where felt needs did not coincide, and analysis untinged with this bland assumption might demonstrate that in some types of cross-class marriage the underlying 'objective' interests of members were at odds with each other.

The discussion could be elaborated further – arguments and counter-arguments have proliferated in recent years – but we think we have said enough to demonstrate that measuring a woman's class independently of her husband's or other male head of household's is desirable in principle if it can be achieved in practice; it prevents premature closure on a range of important theoretical questions. Fuelling the theoretical debate, however, is the enormous technical difficulty of measuring an 'independent' class for all women in a manner which will ensure comparability within and between genders. Attempts to do so are reviewed in the next section.

The technical problems of assigning a class to women

If we accept that it is necessary to incorporate women into class analysis, we are still left with the problem of how this is to be done. Some women – e.g. full-time housewives – are currently without paid employment outside the home. Others may be in paid employment but not at a level compatible with their qualifications or with the place they could achieve in the market if free from domestic responsibilities. This is particularly typical of working wives, who may well be in a lower occupation than they might be able to achieve independently and/or in only part-time occupation. Even the apparently simple case of single women is not so simple in practice, because labour market segregation means that women tend to be clustered in particular occupations. These are themselves clustered into relatively small ranges of the occupational scales which have been developed with men's jobs in mind. This makes fine discrimination difficult and tends to suggest that women are more homogeneous with respect to occupational class than it seems reasonable to assert.

Four basic positions have been taken on how to cope with these problems:

(i) to retain the household (family) as the unit of analysis, but to take the woman's occupational position (and/or other characteristics) into account in determining the household's class position;

(ii) to locate women in the class system by their own paid employment, without reference to the household, thus ensuring that all employed women are treated alike, irrespective of marital status;

(iii) to attempt to develop a measure of 'consumption class' for families which will take account of the influence of all family members on life-style, while simultaneously developing an occupation-based measure of individuals' market position – one which more adequately distinguishes between women's occupations than the conventional scales; or

(iv) to locate women in the class system by taking into account both their paid employment (if any) and their role as unpaid domestic labour.

The problem of allocating women to classes is more a methodological than a theoretical one. However, theoretical positions are involved in the debate as to which of these solutions is to be adopted.

The position that the household should remain the unit of analysis, but with women's employment taken into account in assigning it to a class, has resulted in two distinct 'solutions'. One, the dominance principle (Erikson 1984; Haugh 1973; Goldthorpe and Payne 1986), would in practice make very little difference to conventional practice. The dominance principle enshrines the view that the class of the household should not automatically be determined by the male head of household's position, but rather by the occupation of whichever partner has the highest social class position, provided that this person works full-time and is fully committed to the labour market. In practice, then, the husband's class will determine the class of most households, but in a (non-trivial but small) minority of 'deviant' cases the household might take its class from the wife's occupation.

The other 'solution' from this standpoint is that a joint social class should be computed for the household as a whole by combining the classes of husband and wife, if the wife is economically active (Heath and Britten 1984; Britten and Heath 1983; Pahl and Wallace 1985). A variant which goes further by also giving some weight to characteristics of full-time house-wives would combine a number of possible class indicators – e.g. educational level, housing tenure, etc. as well as occupation (Osborne and Morris 1979).

Osborne and Morris argue that the strength of an index of social class premised on joint characteristics lies in the ability it appears to have of predicting many more social and economic inequalities than simpler measures can. The weakness of one based on occupation alone is that it can be applied straight-forwardly only to those currently in paid employment; others would have to be classified according to a past occupation or the occupation of another person. They also point out the problem of classification in cross-class marriages – it is not immediately clear whether 'husband manual plus wife non-manual' is equal to or different from 'husband non-manual plus wife manual'. They argue that social class is a multifactorial entity and that occupation is only one important aspect. They suggest, there-fore, an alternative social index based on occupational status of head of household, level of education for the partner with the highest qualifications, and housing situation for both, some-times with multiple indicators. Families without an employed head of household were rated zero on occupation but scored on other variables in a trial analysis, and a comparison with families with a male head in employment suggested that the missing occupation did not grossly affect the scale score. Thus it was possible to provide an adequate social rating for families without an employed head. They found in a study of child health that the scale was a better predictor than just using head of house-hold's occupation.

However, the scale devised by Osborne and Morris is not entirely adequate as a way of taking account of women's characteristics in class theory. Their composite index is more like a status ranking of households than a classification of social class, and even when a wife is economically active, her own occupation is not taken into account in determining the household level. Britten and Heath argue for a household classification which does take into account the occupation of both husband and wife: they argue that a wife's occupation makes a demonstrable difference and needs to be taken into account in determining the class position of the household. They recognize the ambiguous class situation of female routine non-manual workers, and in their 1983 paper they argue that regarding women in these occupations as middle class probably leads to overestimation of the number of cross-class marriages; in their 1984 paper, however, they argue that female office workers should be classified as middle class but that sales and service personnel belong in the working class. They suggest a five-way classification incorporating wives' as well as husbands' occupational class in determining household position:

Class I   Husband and wife both in Registrar General's Class
            I or II, or husband in that class and wife a full-time
            housewife, or one partner in that class and the other
            unemployed or absent.
Class II   Husband and wife both in RG class I, II or III (at
            least one in III), or husband in III and wife a full-
            time housewife, or one partner in III and the other
            unemployed or absent.
Class III   Cross-class marriages, not fitting any of these
            categories.
Class IV   Husband and wife in manual occupations, or
            husband in a manual occupation and wife a full-
            time housewife, or one partner in a manual occu-
            pation and the other unemployed or absent.
Class V   Husband and wife unemployed, or one partner
            unemployed and the other absent.

Pahl and Wallace (1985) used a similar joint class classification when looking at the provision for oneself of services that could have been bought on the market and found it a better predictor than husband's class alone.

However, while the use of a joint household classification does take account of a wife's occupational role, it assumes that the existing classification systems are adequate for classifying women's occupations and that there is symmetry within the family. It closes off questions about how husband and wife influence each other's class perceptions and actions, and questions of inequality within the household. Susan McRae (1986) conducted a more detailed study of cross-class families that examined these issues in some depth. She looked at what she refers to as 'genuine' cross-class marriages – such as a marriage where the wife was employed in occupational class I or II and the husband a manual worker. Although she studied only thirty families she found considerable diversity, in terms of the subjective class assignment of these families, in social imagery and in voting behaviour. Only in six families did husband and wife appear to share views – pro-socialist, pro-union positions – but see themselves as middle class. In other marriages the husbands and wives differed at least in some attitudes; in some cases this resulted in conflict, in others in an 'agreement to disagree'. What her study demonstrates is that living together does not automatically result in shared social imagery or shared attitudes towards class action. Another study (Porter 1983), of working-class couples in Bristol, raises similar doubts about the sharing of social imagery in marriage. Given that we cannot assume shared consumption patterns in the family either, as there is often gender asymmetry in this respect (see Jan Pahl 1980, 1983; Young 1952), and given labour market inequalities, the assignment of a joint household class as a predictor of class sentiment or class consciousness begins to appear an exercise of doubtful validity.

An alternative position is to argue that women should be incorporated into class analysis by classifying them on the basis of their own occupations (see, for example, Stanworth 1984). It is argued that a woman's class consciousness and class awareness is more likely to be determined by her own work experience than by that of her husband, and there is indeed empirical evidence for this proposition (Ritter and Hargens 1975; Abbott and Sapsford 1986; Abbott 1987). If women are classified by their own occupation, labour market inequalities and class inequalities are available as topics of investigation, for both men and women, in a way that they are not if any kind of joint classification is used. Studies of social mobility in Britain and the United States (see Chapter 3) have shown that the incorporation of women into the analysis results in important modification of theory. Heath *et al.* (1985) have also shown the importance of classification by own occupation when studying voting behaviour.

Doubts have been raised about the appropriateness of existing class scales, devised for men, as a means of classifying women. It is argued that the existing scales do not differentiate sufficiently between occupations, because of the concentration of women in certain occupational groups that are much more rarely filled by men (Murgatroyd 1982a, 1982b; Arber, Dale, and Gilbert 1986; Roberts 1985, 1986). Murgatroyd argues that gender is of crucial importance in 'placing' people within the occupational hierarchy and shaping the division of labour. She points to the high degree of sex-segregation within the labour market, and argues that most places in the occupational hierarchy are in some sense gendered or carry a 'sex association'. (Even in non-segregated industries, it is not self-evident and sometimes simply not true that the two sexes are equally regarded.) Thus the relationship between occupational class and individual 'marketability' is affected by the gender of the individual, and also by the sexual composition of the occupational group. This calls into question the possibility of distinguishing fixed places within the hierarchy, irrespective of gender. Furthermore, the fact that jobs are seen as 'female' is an important characteristic of those that are. There is, for example, increasing evidence that 'skill' is itself a social construct and that occupations in which men are concentrated are more likely to be regarded as skilled, irrespective of the training actually required for the job and the skills actually necessary to undertake it (Beechey 1984; Coyle 1984; Phillips and Taylor 1980). The strength of male trade unions, and the marginal role of women within unions even when they are members, means that men have successfully excluded women from the apprenticeship schemes that lead to 'skilled' status and have negotiated better wages and working conditions for male than for female workers (Arber, Dale, and Gilbert 1986). While women comprise some 40 per cent of the labour force, they tend to be concentrated in a relatively small number of occupational groups. This labour market segmentation is vertical as well as horizontal – women are concentrated in lower-class occupations (Hakim 1979).

The Registrar General's scale groups together occupations whose holders have 'broadly similar standing' (OPCS 1970), but the similarity is greater for men than for women because a wide variety of women will be aggregated under the one heading. Thus in analysing 1971 Census data, Murgatroyd (1982b) found that while over 50 per cent of women are in non-manual occupations, 39 per cent are in routine ones and only 1 per cent in the category of higher professional and managerial workers. Smilarly, women in manual occupations are concentrated in what is classed as semi- and unskilled work, while men are more likely to be found in the 'skilled' category (see also Arber *et al.* 1986). Furthermore, Arber *et al.* argue that the manual/non-manual divide is of less significance for women than for men; because of their concentration in service work, it is much less easy to assign women to one side or the other of the divide. For example, shop assistants and supermarket check-out girls are in the Registrar General's class IIINM, while telephonists and waitresses are in class IV, which also includes air hostesses. In a given class, women who occupy very different situations may be aggregated together; for example, all nurses are in the same class whether they are untrained auxiliaries or Senior Nursing Officers. Within a given occupational group, the differences between the pay and conditions of men and women are often greater than the differences between manual and non-manual female workers. It is generally assumed that men and women in the same class share a common occupation and a common labour market position. However, the within-class occupational distributions of men and women differ, sometimes quite markedly. For example, 10 per cent of men in the Registrar General's class V are cleaners, compared with 85 per cent of women; men in this class are mostly unskilled labourers, railway porters, dustmen, road workers, road-sweepers, lorry drivers' mates, etc. Finally, the same occupation may have a different meaning and labour market situation for men and women. This is especially the case in clerical work, where for men it may be regarded as a career route to management while women see it as an occupation 'for the duration' – see Crompton and Jones 1984; Llewellyn 1981. (See Attwood and Hatton 1983, for a similar argument with respect to careers in hairdressing.) The fact that some men are intergenerationally counter-mobile but fewer women suggests that this may be the case for other occupations. (Chapter 3 has a discussion of counter-mobility.) It has also been pointed out that existing scales are even less satisfactory for classifying part-time female workers and do not accommodate full-time housewives at all except as economically inactive (i.e. as all in the same 'class' irrespective of their differences).

A number of attempts have been made to develop alternative scales more adequate for measuring the social class of women. Murgatroyd (1982a), for instance, developed a five-point scale by multidimensional scaling of 1971 Census data on couples both of whom were in employment, assuming that husbands and wives shared a life-style and using this assumption to assess the degree of similarity between women in the thirty-nine different socio-economic groups which the Census records. Her scale, the *Women's Social Groups* scale, looks not dissimilar to the Registrar General's on the surface, but it differs a fair amount in detail (see *Table 1*). As Murgatroyd herself realizes, however, the scale cannot be used for classifying full-time housewives, and it fails to distinguish full-time from part-time workers, though the two do not necessarily share a market position. The underlying

Table 1   The Women's Social Groups scale

group	contents
1 Professional	Registrar General (RG) Class 1
2 Employers, managers, and intermediate workers	RG Class II plus self-employed from RG Classes IIINM and IIIM
3 Routine white-collar	Most of RG Class IIINM plus some semi- and unskilled 'own account' workers
4 Personal service and skilled manual workers	Personal service workers from IIINM, IIIM, and IV, plus the remaining skilled workers
5 Semi- and unskilled manual	The remainder of RG Classes IV and V

Source: Murgatroyd (1982a)

assumption is made that family members share a pattern of consumption, and that this pattern can be assumed to run across all employed women in a category, including those not married, which is not an entirely safe assumption. Finally, the scale is not intended to apply to men, so there would be large problems of comparability in research which included both genders.

Another scale which overcomes at least some of these problems by distinguishing full- and part-time work has been developed by Dale, Gilbert, and Arber (1983, 1985). They ranked women's occupations by a series of variables which they argue reflect market power – wage levels, fringe benefits, level of educational qualification typical of the job – and used cluster analysis on 155 occupational groups, separately for full-time and part-time workers, to develop a five-point scale for women in full-time employment and a four-point one for part-time workers (shown in *Table 2*). The scale shows clearly the different market positions of full- and part-time female workers, and the differences between male and female workers. Note also that the skill levels among female manual workers do not hold up in terms of the rewards they receive for their labour, and the absence of fringe benefits among women working in manu-facturing industry is particularly highlighted.

However, this scale can be criticized in the same way as Murgatroyd's. While its construction provides interesting data on labour-market segmentation and the different labour-market positions of males and females and of full- and part-time workers, it is unclear how it could or would be used in research which included samples of both sexes. Furthermore, it is unclear whether the scale is to be regarded as a continuous ranking of prestige, in the United States tradition, or as a categorization of classes in relation to each other, sharing social and economic interests, in the European tradition. In other words (and this point holds for Murgatroyd's scale as well), it is unclear whether the intent is to produce a replacement for the Registrar General's scale or a new scale for women comparable to, for example, the Hope-Goldthorpe scale for men. It seems likely, however, given their arguments in the unpublished 1983 report to the Equal Opportunities Commission, that they are concerned with a classification scale that would enable women's

Table 2   Preliminary Surrey Group classification

full-time scale	part-time scale
1 *Professional* schoolteachers, managers of nurses, lecturers, social workers, professional workers	*professional* primary and secondary teachers
2 *technical and supervisory* supervisors and managers of clerks, office workers or typists, police officers, nurses	*clerical and technical* typists and secretaries, nurses, clerks and cashiers, office machine operators, hairdressers, paramedical and laboratory assistants
3 *clerical workers, etc.* E.g. clerks, cashiers, typists, secretaries, telephone operators, sales managers (large firms), bus conductors, etc.	*personal service workers* E.g. cleaners, charwomen, canteen assistants, maids, kitchen hands, barmaids, storekeepers, cooks, laundresses, service workers NEC, printing workers NEC, hospital orderlies, etc.
4 *service and productive workers* E.g. assemblers, machine tool operators, barmaids, canteen assistants, shop assistants	*manual workers in manufacturing and shop workers*
5 *manual workers in manufacturing*	

Source: Dale, Gilbert, and Arber (1985)

occupational class to be recorded more adequately in official statistics.

In a more recent paper also derived in part from the 1983 report (Arber, Dale, and Gilbert 1986) the Surrey Group report on the development of a Surrey Occupational Class Scale intended for use to categorize both men and women but discriminating as finely as possible between the occupational sectors in which women are mostly employed. They suggest that the occupation of women in full-time employment is a good indicator of market position but are more doubtful about part-time workers, given the tendency of women to take part-time work at a lower level than their previous class on return to the labour market. For full-time housewives they argue, on the basis of Martin and Roberts (1984), that the best indicator would be last full-time occupation prior to the birth of the first child, and failing this then just last full-time occupation.

Listed below is their nine-point classification (Dale, Gilbert, and Arber 1983; Arber, Dale, and Gilbert 1986), which they suggest more adequately differentiates between women's occupations than do existing scales and can still be used for men's as well.

1 Higher professional
2 Employers and managers
3 Lower professional
4 Secretarial and clerical
5 Foremen and self-employed manual workers
6 Shop and personal service workers
7 Skilled manual workers
8 Semi-skilled manual workers
9 Unskilled manual workers

They do admit, however, that despite their attempts at disaggregation, 39 per cent of full-time working women still fall in one of their classes, SOC 4. They argue, however, that

'The two main advantages of [The Surrey Occupational Classification] for women are, first, it provides a distinction, blurred in both RG classes and collapsed SEGs, between employers and managers (SOC 2) and lower professional (SOC 3). SOC 2 is predominantly male, containing 13 per cent of full-time men compared to five per cent of full-time women and under two per cent of part-time working women, and SOC 3 is predominantly female, containing 13 per cent of full-time women compared to only 5 per cent of men. Secondly, it separates shop workers (SOC 6) from secretarial/clerical workers and sales representatives (SOC 4) and separates personal service workers (SOC 6) from semiskilled factory workers (SOC 8). These two changes highlight the concentration of part-time women in shop and personal service work, 35 per cent compared to 14 per cent of full-time women and a bare 3 per cent of men. They also show clearly the smaller participation of part-time women in clerical and secretarial occupations which is masked in other classifications.

Under 20 per cent of part-time working women are in SOC 4 compared with 33 per cent in RG class IIINM and 44 per cent in collapsed SEG 3.   (p. 68)

They checked the validity of the scale by tabulating it against income separately for men, full-time women workers, and part-time women and found that the gradient of income by class was equally strong for men and women. The expected gradient was found for men and full-time women, but part-time female employees in manual, shop, or personal service work broke the pattern, all appearing equally disadvantaged.

What they have constructed is a classification that distinguishes occupational categories which are distinct in terms of work and market situation. However, this does not necessarily mean that it will distinguish between individuals in terms of life-style because, as they themselves argue, life-style has to be measured in terms of households. Certainly this scale seems to overcome many of the problems associated with the conventional scales, with the one developed by Murgatroyd or with the previous one from the Surrey Group. While the Surrey Group suggest a way in which full-time housewives can be assigned a class, this itself suggests that current work experience is not what shapes class position, action, and consciousness for full-time housewives – and they themselves are surprised at this outcome (see Dale, Gilbert, and Arber 1983). Housewives are effectively classified on the highest position held; why not others? The joint scale does not fully take account of the way that the same occupation may have a different meaning and lead to different experiences for men and for women who hold it. Also, as with the other scales discussed, it is not clear what it means to say that a group of people share a common market class. Does it mean just that they share similar rewards for their labour, different from those received in other classes? Or are they suggesting that sharing a market position entails shared social and economic interests that are different from and/or in conflict with those of other classes – as, for example, with the Hope-Goldthorpe Scale. It is not yet clear from the work of the Surrey group what the answers to these questions are. The scale looks promising for future research, but its basis still needs some clarification.

One area that needs considerable clarification is the relationship between 'market' class and 'consumption' class – the former being the relationship of the individual to the labour market and the latter the relationship of the family to the market in goods and services. Dale *et al*. argue that

> 'The consumption class of the family represents all the effects of the accumulated inputs from all members of the family, either in terms of wages or in domestic labour, as well as patterns of expenditure it adopts.' (1983: 7)

Consumption class is seen as shared by all family members, and it was determined in the research by a continuous composite of fourteen related variables covering housing, possession of consumer durables, family income, etc. They took into account the family structure (whether single or a couple, and whether the household had children); they also took stage of 'family life-cycle' into account, distinguishing families, for example, by whether they were currently rearing children, had already finished doing so or had not yet started. They concluded that husbands' and wives' occupational class (using the Surrey Occupational Classification for both) had an effect on family income and the composite life-style variable, as did family structure and stage in family life-cycle. Furthermore, the contribution a full-time housewife makes to her family life-style varies with her past occupation. (They recognize that their measure of consumption or life-style class is at best tentative and that the variables included might not be available in most research. They point out, however, that Fox and Goldblatt (1982) suggest that the greatest discrimination is obtained by using occupation to indicate market class and housing tenure to indicate consumer class.)

The Surrey Group found a high correlation between market and consumer class for men, but this did not hold up for married women in full- or part-time employment. They leave unresolved the relationship of the two measures of class and their use in empirical research.

> 'We have not pursued our original intention of following Britten and Heath (1983) in producing a joint classification of husbands' and wives' occupations since their work makes the

assumption that there is a direct additive relationship between the occupation of individuals and the life-style,
consumption patterns and voting behaviour of the family. We
have argued that it is useful to make a conceptual distinction
between the occupational class of the individual and the
consumption class of the family and that although there will
be a strong association between the two, the extent and
nature of this association should be a matter for empirical
investigation.'   (1983: 106)

Until this further research has been undertaken it seems that the
allocation of a class position to a woman that reflects both her
market situation and her consumption class remains problematic. We would expect that the two aspects of a woman's life
would articulate with each other in forming her class attitudes,
class awareness, and class action, but we accept that further
research will be needed to determine the form of such
articulation. Dale, Gilbert, and Arber have certainly demonstrated that allocating a woman a class position on the basis of
her husband's occupation is a poor indicator of her market class,
and that a woman's market class influences the consumption
class of her family. They also demonstrate, however, the
inherent difficulty of allocating women (or, indeed, men,
though the point is seldom considered) a class position that
adequately reflects their total class situation.

A major criticism of scales so far developed, from a feminist
perspective, is their failure to include full-time housewives,
taking account of unpaid work performed in the patriarchal
mode of production – although Dale, Gilbert, and Arber (1983)
are well aware of the contribution made by full-time housewives
to the consumption class of their families. Helen Roberts (1985,
1986, 1987) and her colleagues at the Social Statistics Research
Unit of City University are in the process of constructing a class
scale for women which would distinguish between women's
jobs and between full- and part-time work, allocate a class
position to full-time housewives, and be a measure of both
market and life-style class position. The City Classification
Scheme is being constructed following analysis of a 1 per cent
sample of the 1981 Census. Roberts has subdivided the 44
occupational groups in which women most commonly figure

into four sub-groups according to domestic responsibilities and whether employment is full- or part-time. Those in other occupational groups (17 per cent of the sample) have been divided into five residual groups, each similarly subdivided, and women not in paid employment have been divided into five groups on the basis of age of youngest child (if any). This gives 201 cells in an initial classification. Having ranked the women in these on the basis of housing tenure and occupational class of husband, Roberts has constructed a provisional hierarchical ordering and is beginning to suggest ways of dividing up the scale to yield class categories.

The major advantage of this classification, when it is developed, will be that it will enable all women to be allocated *their own* class position on the basis of a fairly small number of questions. (Roberts recognizes that domestic responsibilities other than child-care will eventually have to be included.) Quite how it will develop is not yet clear, but one problem we can foresee is that the class of women not in employment is based on husband's occupational group and housing tenure (plus domestic responsibilities), which may mask inequalities between full-time housewives. Another is that at present it resembles an American prestige scale more than a European class categorization. Also, while it does not assume shared patterns of consumption or life-style within households, it does assume that husband's contributions can be 'averaged'. It could be, however, that the sort of man a woman marries, according to her occupation, is an important class marker. Some evidence for this proposition comes from Prandy (1986): air hostesses, for instance, marry 'higher class' husbands than waitresses, although both share a Registrar General's classification category. Finally, as with Murgatroyd's scale or the earlier Surrey one, Roberts' scale is for use only with women.

We accept that there are many problems with the existing class scales and the ways in which individuals are allocated to a class position. We are not yet convinced, however, that any of the alternative scales developed to date have solved these problems (though the scales developed by Roberts and by the Surrey Group look promising). One major problem is the necessity for a distinction between market and lifestyle class position, and the consequent question of how these two relate to each other and combine to determine an individual's class location. Another is the extent to which we have to assume that members of a household share, not only lifestyle, but also class attitudes, values, and orientation. These are empirical questions that need far more investigation. However, it should be noted that they are not just problems of *women's* class; the class position of men is equally problematic, and for the same reasons. Moreover, where women and men live together we need to investigate how they influence each other and how household, as opposed to individual, experiences and patterns of work influence the lifestyle of all members of the family and their class attitudes. This research has begun (Britten and Heath 1983; Heath and Britten 1984; McRae 1986; Porter 1983), and the indication so far is that partners do indeed have an influence on each other; whether that influence is symmetrical, however, cannot yet be said.

Conclusions

We have argued, then, that there is increasing empirical evidence to suggest that for sociologists to ignore women's class position is unwise – and that this holds even if the research is primarily concerned with men. As Chapman (1984) has argued, a wife's social class needs to be taken into account in explaining her husband's intragenerational mobility; her ability to take on the lifestyle of a higher class may be crucial in his ability to be upwardly mobile. Also the fact that married women tend to 'be employed' rather than 'have careers' is crucial in explaining male mobility. Dual-career families are a rarity; generally one partner (the male) has a career while the other (generally the wife) has at best a good steady job. Janet Finch (1983) has documented the importance of a wife's unpaid labour for many men, in enabling the men to carry out the duties and obligations of their occupations. In order to develop class theory and class analysis it is therefore vital that women are incorporated and that account is taken of their unpaid work in the patriarchal mode of production as well as of their paid labour.

The problems of incorporating women are considerable, however, as we have seen. These problems are not problems of gender; they are the problems of incorporating the economically inactive, those who have a transitory participation in the labour market, those who have interrupted careers, those who are intragenerationally downwardly mobile, and those who live in a household of which they are not the head. It is a contingent fact that these qualities are particularly typical of women at present. With increased levels of male unemployment and an increase in part- as opposed to full-time employment these same problems are coming to the surface in analysing the class position of men as well. The question of the use of the household as a unit of analysis is also an interesting one. We, in common with much of the literature, have tended to use 'household' and 'family' as equivalent terms. 'Household', however, is a technical term and refers to a group of people who live together. In most research one of these people is selected as 'the head', and his or her occupation is used as a basis for classifying the others. Wives are, of course, the largest single group whose class is determined, but there are other groups similarly placed – young people still living with their parents, for example, who are equally assumed to have a derived class position, and possibly with as little justification.

While the theoretical debate about the incorporation of women into class analysis has been going on – and, as we have argued above, these are important questions for class theory generally, and not just 'women's questions' – empirical research has also been taking place. Most of the research has been small-scale and ethnographic in nature, frequently studies of working-class women, looking at class-awareness and orientation. Even a partial and incomplete catalogue would have to mention Porter 1983; McRae 1986; Hunt 1980; Webb 1985; Westwood 1984; Cavendish 1982; Coyle 1984. These studies have enabled us to develop a greater understanding of the 'female prism', how women relate to class and gender inequalities, and to some extent of the relationship between men and women. However, the commitment of many feminists to qualitative research and, we suspect, the difficulties women researchers have in acquiring large research grants have been a barrier to progress. Larger-scale, more quantitatively based research is essential for the development of a more general picture of women's social class position, to see how incorporating women enables us to understand better not just class structure but also awareness, consciousness, and action. The rest of this book is intended to make a small contribution to this endeavour by providing the sort of information on women and their social imagery that has previously been available only for men. We realize that our analysis is at best a start in this direction, and that it is based on a 'conventional' classification scheme which can be validly and heavily criticized (see Chapter 2). However, we feel that one of the necessary steps is providing information on women comparable with that which is available for men. We hope that this analysis may assist in determining the way forward – for example, by showing whether women share the same social imagery as men in the same occupational class, to what extent factors such as education and husband's class are important in shaping a woman's social imagery, whether, even, the social imagery of single, married and widowed, or divorced women is similar or different. The answers to these questions will enable us to begin to see what the influences on social imagery *are* for women – occupation, or education, or husband's occupation – in so far as we can tell from a questionnaire firmly grounded in malestream class literature. Indeed, it is probable that we should be asking the same questions about men: is their social imagery really determined entirely by occupation, or are other factors also important? In other words the questions raised in this chapter and the rest of the book apply equally to men and to women. The feminist critiques of stratification and class theory suggest that theory is in crisis, and not just because it appears inadequate for analysing women's class position, but because it ignores the private sphere and its changing impact on both genders and assumes that the workplace is an autonomous and controlling influence on *men's* lives. Not only do we challenge the theoretical assumption that married women – and by extension all women – have a derived class position and by implication derived social imagery, but also that men's social class and social imagery can be seen as independent and not in the slightest influenced by the women with whom they live.

2 The data base

The Survey

The People in Society Questionnaire was devised by Jane Henry for use on Open University course DE304 'Research Methods in Education and the Social Sciences', an honours-level course in methods which involves substantial amounts of student project work; it was also used on DE801 'An MSc in Advanced Research Methods' when the latter was developed. (For full details of the construction, piloting, and operation of the survey, see Henry 1979, 1981.) The questionnaire has been administered annually since 1979, with each of the two courses' nationally distributed students collecting four cases according to an interlocking quota scheme which is described below. The data used in this book are drawn from the years 1980–1984 and comprise 5,261 cases – 2,628 males, 2,630 females, and 3 cases where gender was not coded.

The questionnaire contains a mixture of open-ended and pre-structured questions – the latter tending on the whole to follow the former, to avoid imposing researchers' preconceptions on the informants – on consciousness of, and beliefs about, social class, attitude items related to social class, semantic differential scales to elicit 'images' or 'stereotypes' of the middle and the working class and to locate self-image with respect to them, and demographic information about age, education, employment, and the employment of the head of household. Many of the questions are along the same lines as or are derived from those asked in earlier research, so that a replication of previous conclusions would be possible, but to the best of our knowledge measures such as the semantic differentials have not been used before in this research context. The initial questionnaire, a mix of well-tried discriminating variables with new questions, was first piloted by thirty-two interviews split between an older town in Derbyshire, a new town in the Midlands, and an area in the Surrey 'commuter belt'. Despite the fact that the pilot sample turned out to be atypical in ways which should have exaggerated class differences – weighted towards the professional and managerial middle class, on the one hand, and the Labour-voting working class, on the other – many of the originally planned attitude statements on, for example, educational aspirations, job opportunities, and attitude to work had to be dropped because they were clearly failing to discriminate between middle- and working-class informants. A second pilot yielding 67 usable cases was conducted in a mix of urban and rural areas scattered throughout England, on a revised questionnaire. This led to questions being rephrased to clarify their meaning, or unalterably ambiguous items being dropped. Further items which produced highly skewed distributions, failed to discriminate between classes or appeared to be producing large numbers of 'don't know' responses were also dropped, given that there were limitations on the number of variables that could be included on the data base. The pilot data were also used as a basis for constructing coding frames for the open-ended questions.

The main strength of this survey for our current purposes is its size. We know of no other available data base which contains responses from several thousand women on whether they work, for how long, what they earn, what their husband earns (if they have one), the class of job which they (and husbands) have, their educational level, and their views and attitudes on social class. The data were collected over a number of years from all regions of the United Kingdom – including Scotland, Wales and Northern Ireland – by a wide range of interviewers no one of whom has contributed more than a minuscule proportion to the total. The likelihood of deliberate interviewer biases is therefore not high.

Its weaknesses, which will be discussed in more detail below, stem from five sources:

(i) sampling – quota sampling, which was the only approach practical for national student use, is prone to selection biases within cells of the quotas (and indeed several have been detected and are outlined below);

(ii) limitations on the amount of data which could be stored and made available to students for remote computer analysis via telephone links meant that some potentially interesting variables had to be discarded;

(iii) for the same reason some of the data have had to be 'degraded' more then one would have liked in the interests of compact storage – for example, we have the occupational class of respondents but not actual jobs or professions;

(iv) the scale used for the coding of social class, which was designed for categorizing men's jobs, is not a good instrument for use with women's (see Chapter 1);

(v) interviewers were not professionals but students, which could be said to entail the risk of further error variance in the coded responses.

The last of these weaknesses is, we think, compensated for by strengths in the design of the survey and the range of types of people used as interviewers. The other four will on occasion limit the interpretability of some of the data and should be borne in mind in later chapters, but we do not regard them as fatal weaknesses.

The data

The People in Society questionnaire starts with five questions carefully constructed to elicit self-assigned class with a minimum of prompting or imposition of researchers' categories. They range from Q.1 'Do you see yourself as belonging to any particular group in society?' through increasingly specific questions using the concept of social class, to Q.5 'If you had to say you were either middle or working class, which would you say?' At each stage respondents have the opportunity to 'drop out' from further questions by denying that social class is a meaningful concept for them, but in fact a majority mentioned class spontaneously in response to the first of these questions, and virtually everyone was prepared to place himself or herself in the middle or working class in response to the directive Question 5. These questions are followed by four more which try to tap the meaning of the concept 'social class' for the respondent. Questions 6 and 7 ask 'What do you mean when you talk about . . . ' the middle and the working class, Question 8 asks which of a list of factors – occupation, lifestyle, education, wealth, manner, income, etc. – are most important and next most important in determining a person's class, and Question 9 offers a list of six job positions – foreman, wages clerk, typist, tobacconist, saleswoman (in a department store), and car mechanic – to be judged as on the whole working class or middle class. Finally in this explicitly class-related section of the questionnaire respondents are asked what political party they usually vote for or support at general elections, and to choose between sets of 'attitude statements', modelled on previous research into class images, which will be discussed in the appropriate chapters below.

Next follow three pages each containing fourteen semantic differential items – rich *vs* poor, plans ahead *vs* lives for the present, reckless *vs* cautious, friendly *vs* unfriendly, etc. – which are to be filled in by each respondent on seven-point scales ranging from 'extremely x' to 'extremely not-x'. The first page asks respondents to say that 'The kind of person who is *working class* is . . . ' somewhere on the seven-point scale with respect to each of the adjectives, the second page deals similarly with the middle class, and on the third page they are invited to say that 'I am . . . ', describing themselves in similar terms. Jane Henry derived two 'subscales' from the pilot study data – a 'situation in life' factor loading most heavily on rich/poor and successful/ unsuccesful but also loading on items to do with conventional success such as planning ahead, education, intelligence, and a 'character' factor loading for middle class on, for example, cautious, cold, unfriendly, saves, while working class loaded on, for example, impulsive, warm, friendly, spends. Statistical analysis replicated on successive samples suggests that the subscales are reasonably distinct and reasonably stable over time, and that individual responses of the working- and middle-class items correlate negatively with corresponding items for the other class.

Finally come fourteen demographic items: marital status, age (grouped), age at which full-time education was terminated, highest qualification obtained, whether the respondent is currently working (full- or part-time), and if not whether retired, temporarily unemployed, or unemployed for two years or more, main occupation if working or recently unemployed, father's occupation (current or most recent), whether the respondent is the head of household, occupation of the head of household, the respondent's and head of household's annual income, nationality (British or other), gender, and Open University teaching region. Various recodings were carried out on these data before the current analysis was undertaken:

(i) Obvious breaks in consistency were restored – for example, if the respondent is coded as head of household but head of household's income has not been entered, then respondent's income would be inserted.

(ii) Answers to the question 'At what age did you complete your full-time education?' were recomputed taking into account date of birth – roughly computable from current age and year of survey – and the known dates on which the minimum school-leaving age has been raised, to yield a new variable indicating years of *post-compulsory* schooling (coded as none, 1, or 2+).

(iii) The two income variables were adjusted to take account of wage inflation by expressing them in 1984 values.

Occupations – own, father's and head of household's – were classified on a six-point scale using the Social Grading Scheme, a modification of the Registrar General's classification widely used in market research. The six-fold classification is shown as *Table 3*. (The problems of this classification scheme for dealing with women's occupations – and the problems of other more sophisticated scales – have already been discussed in Chapter 1.

Table 3   The Social Grading Scheme classification

grade	description
A	higher managerial and professional
B	lower managerial and professional
C1	supervisory, lower, and routine non-manual
C2	foremen, skilled manual
D	semi-skilled and unskilled manual
E	not economically active

This survey at least does not adopt the common practice of assuming that a whole household is correctly placed by the class of the (male) head of household, which is what makes it a useful one for the current analysis.) The categories are often grouped further into a two-fold classification, ABC1 being referred to as middle-class and C2D as working-class. (Category E cannot be accommodated within this collapsed classification, as it is made up of a variety of totally disparate 'inactive' groups, including the unemployed, the retired, and housewives.)

This classification, along with the Registrar General's, has a number of shortcomings for sociological analysis. Nichols (1979) has noted that it is essentially made up of descriptive categories relating to a status hierarchy, with the implicit assumption that there is general agreement on the ordering of categories. Individuals are categorized according to occupation alone; the ranking is based on the general standing of occupational groups within the community. Thus the categorization does not explain the generation of inequalities in the structural dynamic of society; rather, it describes its results.

The last of these criticisms can equally be made of what Nichols refers to as sociological definitions of class – that is, those derived from the work of Max Weber. The most recent schema developed in this tradition is the one developed for the Oxford Mobility Study (Goldthorpe 1980) and used in modified form in the Scottish Mobility Study (Chapman 1984). As with the social grading scheme, occupation is used to place an individual or household in a social class, but the categories are different and it is argued that the relation between them does not necessarily have to be conceived as hierarchical. The classification's categories are given below.

   (i) Higher-grade professional, managers, and large proprietors
  (ii) Lower-grade professional and managers
 (iii) Routine non-manual workers
 (iv) Small proprietors and the self-employed
  (v) Foremen and technicians
 (vi) Skilled manual workers
(vii) Semi-skilled and unskilled manual workers

The major difference between this and the social grading scheme lies in the separate classification of the lesser bourgeoisie (included in C1 or C2 in the Social Grading Scheme) and of foremen and technicians (included in C2 in the Social Grading Scheme). The main argument for this is that the economic interests of these groups could well be different from those associated with other occupations with which other classification schemes would include them. However, the collapsed version of this scale includes these two groups with routine non-manual workers as an 'intermediate' class, and it is therefore possible to derive a comparable classification from the social grading scheme (see *Table 4*) – the major difference being that self-employed manual workers and foremen have to be included in the working class rather than the intermediate class.

Heath *et al*. (1985), in their study of 1983 General Election data, argue that it is vital in analysis to separate out the petty bourgeoisie and foremen and technicians from routine non-manual workers and the working class, again on the grounds that they have different economic interests, and despite the fact that their incomes may be comparable or even lower. In their study they used another collapsed version of the Oxford Mobility Classification (see *Table 5*) and found that in terms of

Table 4 Collapsed Oxford Mobility Study scale and a comparable version of the Social Grading Scheme

class	Oxford Mobility Survey	Social Grading Scheme
service	I and II	A and B
intermediate	III, IV, and V	C1
working	VI and VII	C2 and D

Table 5 Modified version of the Oxford scale used by Heath, Jowell, and Curtice (1985)

	classes	percentages of population	
		men %	*women* %
salariat	I and II	30	23
routine non-manual	III	11	46
petty bourgeoisie	IV	10	4
foremen and technicians	V	11	2
working class	VI and VII	38	25

Reprinted with permission from Heath, A., Jowell, R., and Curtice, J. *How Britain votes*, copyright 1985, Pergamon Books Ltd.

political and economic attitudes these two groups could be distinguished from both the traditional working class and other non-manual groups. (Roberts *et al.* also found that the non-manual petty bourgeoisie displayed more conservative values and had different social imagery from both new middle class and routine non-manual workers.) However, the proportions of the Health *et al.* sample who were women in employment and fell into one of these two intermediate groups were very small.

Thus while recognizing the limitations of the social grading scheme, we feel that it is as adequate as any other mainstream classification for the purpose for which we wish to use it – analysing women's social and occupational class in a form comparable with the mainstream analysis of men. In common with much previous research we shall generally collapse the categories into middle-class (A B C1) and working-class (C2 D). In some parts of the analysis we shall separate out C1, given that, for women at least, it has been argued that some of the occupations which fall into this grouping should be reclassified as working-class (Crompton and Jones 1984; Britten and Heath 1983) and that there is some evidence (Holland 1981) that working-class girls regard routine non-manual work as the equivalent for girls of skilled manual work for boys.

The Sample

The sample, as we said above, was drawn by quota methods. Each year each of the *c.* 250 students on the two courses found four respondents to fit half of the 8-cell quota by age, sex, and class outlined in *Table 6*; which half of the eight cells he or she looked for was determined randomly. Quota samples have some merit in terms of speed and cheapness, and in political opinion polls they have almost superseded true random samples (see McKee 1981). Selection biases will almost certainly creep in, however, depending on the nature of the interviewing force, and these can make precise generalization to the population difficult. Compared with Census data, for example, the distributions in the current sample do not match population distributions on either age or class (*Table 7*), as would be expected from the fact that the sample strata were not made proportionate to the distribution of the variables in the population. We have more younger women than the Census

Table 6 Interlocking quota design for the survey

sex	age	class	sample
Male	18–34	ABC1	a
		C2DE	b
	35+	ABC1	b
		C2DE	a
Female	18–34	ABC1	b
		C2DE	a
	35+	ABC1	a
		C2DE	b

Note
Students collected the four cases labelled either a or b, according to a random
selection mechanism.

Table 7 Age and class distributions among the women in the
People in Society Survey, compared with the general population
(%)

	survey	*general population*[1]
age	%	%
18–24	20.3	17.6
25–34	32.1	23.8
35–44	22.9	20.2
45–54[2]	14.6	19.0
55–64[2]	10.2	19.4
class[3]	%	%
A	1.8	1.0
B	21.7	21.1
C1	36.9	40.3
C2	13.4	8.6
D[4]	26.3	28.9
class of husband[5]	%	%
A	11.6	5.4
B	31.9	23.7
C1	13.0	10.5
C2	32.0	38.2
D[4]	11.4	22.3

1 Data on the general population derived from OPCS (1983a), Table 1 [age];
  OPCS (1983b), Table 50 [class]; OPCS (1983b), Table 49 [class of husband].
2 Age 65+ omitted because of disparities between survey and Census on the
  coding of employment status for retired persons.
3 Own occupation
4 Class E omitted because of similar disparities for unemployed persons as for 2.
5 For married women

would predict, and more in class A or B on the basis of own occupation (but fewer in C1). Even within the cells of the quota some sampling biases have crept in, however. We have an excess of Class B women at the expense of C1 in the younger age group, and also a marked excess of Class C2 at the expense of D; in the older age group there is also an excess of C2 at the expense of D, and rather more women in Class A than would be expected.

Looking at key variables which did not form part of the quota design, the distribution of 'husband's class' for married women does not match the Census figures at all closely (see the last block of *Table 7*): we have too many husbands in Class A, B, or (to a lesser extent) C1, rather too few in C2, and far too few in Class D. We also have fewer married women than population figures would suggest even after correction is made for age and class imbalances (though Census definitions place the 'separated' in the 'married' category, while our survey places them with the widowed and divorced, which may go some way towards explaining the disparity). We have more women with educational qualifications (*Table 8*), more working married women (*Table 9*), and among them more women working full time (though again differences in interviewer instruction may go some way towards explaining the disparity).

These sampling biases will be noted where they are important, and figures are corrected for them where we purport to describe the distribution of some trait in the general population.

Table 8   Level of female education: People in Society survey compared with General Household Survey[1]

level of education	People in Society Survey	General Household Survey
	%	%
Less than 'O' level or equivalent	30	56
'O' level or equivalent	23	25
'A' level or equivalent	10	3
Less than degree	12	10
Degree or higher	17	5
Other	3	8

1 Figures derived from an average of two years of GHS data – OPCS (1982 and 1985)

Table 9 Employment status of married women: People in Society Survey compared with Census data (%)[1]

	People in Society Survey	Census
Non-working	28.2	56.4
Employed		
full-time	41.1 (57.2)[2]	22.0 (50.5)[2]
part-time	30.7	21.6

1 Derived from OPCS (1984), Table 1.
2 Figure in brackets represents % of those in employment.

On the whole, they make very little difference to the analysis, for we are remarkably rarely concerned with the distribution of traits in the population. Most of our analysis concerns the interrelationship of traits, attitudes, and/or demographic characteristics, and the question of whether or not the sample is directly representative of the population does not enter into the argument. Only occasionally will it matter that our sample is under- or over-provided with, for example, educationally unqualified or qualified women, and such occasions will be noted as they occur.

It is, of course, a further problem of quota samples that they are not strictly amenable to inferential statistics in the same way as true random samples, because lack of inbuilt biases cannot be guaranteed. We have used conventional tests of significance in the chapters which follow, but they should be interpreted with caution.

One final characteristic of the People in Society Survey was that the interviewers were by and large not experienced at survey work. They were not without training: a good proportion of the course material dealt with theoretical aspects of survey interviewing, the Survey Project Guides constituted a fairly detailed briefing on how the questionnaire was to be administered, and this was backed up by a television programme on how and when to prompt and by *ad hoc* face-to-face sessions run by local tutors. None the less, the interviewers *were* students, not professional interviewers. However, one might say that their 'amateur status' was compensated for in practice by their diversity of academic and personal backgrounds. Most of them were in the Open University's equivalent of the final year of their degree, and their backgrounds were very diverse – from teachers and other professionals taking the degree for career reasons, through clerks and civil servants taking the opportunity of degree-level study, professional women using their studies as a way of breaking back in to the job market after having and rearing children, to housewives and others taking a degree for interest and pleasure. The MSc course, which has run since 1981, attracts a very similar range of people, but with the additional proviso that all would already have good honours degrees and that most would be seriously intending to go on with research of their own. The range of social and academic skills available in the People in Society interview force probably far outstrips those to be found in the conventional interviewing organization, therefore, and we feel little need to apologize for the competence of our interviewers.

3 Social mobility

Introduction

Since the Second World War there has been considerable interest in social mobility studies, which describe movement from one stratum/class to another either intergenerationally or intragenerationally. *Inter*generational mobility studies are concerned with movements in class position between generations, most usually comparing a son's occupational position with that of his father; *intra*generational studies are concerned with movements during an individual's own lifetime. Neither kind, however, is concerned solely or even primarily with description, but rather with the testing of theories about the structure of society. The early study by Glass (1954), for example, was concerned with the openness of British society – to what extent social class/occupational status was inherited. In the United States there has also been great interest in rates of social mobility and the extent to which high mobility rates might be seen as legitimating liberal democracy and thus ensuring overall social stability. The recent Oxford and Scottish Mobility Studies have also been concerned with the openness of society and the extent to which modern Britain has become a meritocracy following the 1944 Education Act.

The primary concern of the Oxford Mobility Study (Goldthorpe *et al.* 1980), however, was to test theoretical propositions derived from the work of Marx and Weber. There were three theories of social mobility and class formation with which the study was particularly concerned:

(i) The first was the 'social closure' thesis (associated with, for example, Giddens 1973: 164–201; Bottomore 1964: Ch. 4; Miliband 1969: 36–45 and 59–67) which argues that those who occupy 'superior positions' may be presumed to be strongly motivated to retain these positions for themselves and their children and to close off access to them by those from lower social classes, and that they have command of the necessary resources to do so.

(ii) The second is the 'buffer-zone' thesis (associated with Parkin 1972: 25, 49–60; Giddens 1973: 108, 181–82, 231; Bottomore 1964: 38–41; Westergaard and Resler 1975: 297–302) which argues that the existence of a high degree of mobility around the manual/non-manual boundary will serve to block off longer-range mobility (and, again, secure overall social closure). Equally as important for testing this thesis as intergenerational mobility is an examination of work-life history – that is, *intra*generational mobility.

(iii) The third is the 'counterbalance' thesis (associated with Westergaard and Little 1967; Westergaard 1972; Westergaard and Resler 1975; Parkin 1972) which argues that with the increased professionalization, bureaucratization, and technological complexity of work, education is the main route to social mobility, and that intragenerational work progress is of little significance. That is, it is no longer the case that men are able to achieve significant mobility via achievement at work; rather, placement in the occupational market is primarily determined by educational qualification.

Social mobility studies have been criticized from a range of theoretical perspectives. Marxists, for example, have questioned the utility of the whole exercise, arguing that whether or not individual mobility is possible, the basic structure of capitalist society remains the same (e.g. Poulantzas 1975). Other Marxists – e.g. Westergaard and Resler (1975) – while agreeing that the major class division in capitalist society is between the proletariat and the bourgeoisie, would none the less see mobility studies as having some importance in terms of understanding why bonds of class solidarity have not developed. Marx, after all, had recognized that such mobility was inimical to the process of class formation. Nichols (1981) points to the way in which bourgeois writers and politicians can use the findings of social mobility studies to mislead and to suggest that Britain is a more 'open' society than is the case in reality; nevertheless he maintains that empirical studies of mobility are of importance because:

'It is in large part rewarding to see men as the "bearers" of a system of structural relationships which is not reducible to a series of interpersonal ones, but there is no warrant in this for the view that the social origins, the mobility – the *experience* of "agents", of living men and women with their own histories – can have no effect on the way they actually bear the weight of the structures in which they are implicated.'   (p. 26)

Nevertheless, as Johnstone and Rattanis (1981) have pointed out, it is true that studies such as the Oxford Mobility Study exclude such important areas as the distribution of wealth, capitalism as a structured relationship of exploitation, and the existence of a 'capitalist class' standing in a distinct position within the 'occupational' structure.

The criticism that is of special relevance in the context of this book is the virtual exclusion of women from social mobility studies. It is true that Glass collected data on women, but these have never been analysed. Since the early 1970s a number of studies in the United States have examined various aspects of female social mobility, but there has been no *major* study among them, the results have been published only in journal articles, and it is not necessarily the case that the results of these surveys are generalizable to Britain. The Oxford Mobility Study excluded women (except for data on wives' marital mobility) on both practical and theoretical grounds, and while the Scottish Mobility Study did include a sub-sample of wives, to date only one paper has been published on this aspect of the study. (Also, given the sampling methods, only married women were included, and these were sampled on the basis of their husbands' occupations.)

We have already seen in Chapter 1 that one of the major justifications for excluding women from research in the area of social class has been that the family is the unit of stratification and that the class/status position of the household is determined by the occupation of its (male) head. The Oxford Mobility Study gives this as one reason for excluding women. Other reasons which may have been more decisive were financial constraints coupled with a perceived need to replicate earlier studies – funds were not available both to draw the size of male sample necessary for replication of important earlier studies and to draw an independent female sample as well. (As Hindess (1981) points out, however, why replication was considered so necessary is unclear, as of the two major reports published, one (Halsey *et al.* 1981) is critical of the decision not to sample females as well as males, and the other (Goldthorpe *et al.* 1980) does not in fact include a full replication of the major studies the researchers set out to replicate.) Goldthorpe's final argument is that women were excluded because for the period under consideration the majority of women had not been economically active outside the home, and those who were had only been intermittently employed, generally in part-time work. (This may be true of *married* women, but it is not true of women as a whole, who have formed 30 per cent of the workforce since at least the 1911 Census.)

A number of general points can be made in contradiction of Goldthorpe *et al.* which stress the importance of considering patterns of female mobility. If the concern is with the openness of society and the extent to which individuals can be mobile within the class structure then it would seem just as important to look at female as at male mobility. By not including women, sex-related occupational demarcations are ignored, as is the articulation between class background, gender, and education in individual mobility. As far as class formation goes, the mobility of women is also of fundamental importance, whether the individual or the household is seen as the fundamental unit of stratification and independently of how a woman's class is determined in practice (by her own occupation or that of her husband). Marital mobility, for example, is of vital interest – how many women marry men up or down the class hierarchy, or at the same level, and how this influences class formation given the possibility of familial ties across classes. For that matter, what is the influence of *male* marital mobility? If the unit of stratification is taken as the family, a wife's occupational role may be of vital interest in that it may enable a family to enjoy a materially higher standard of living and influence the attitudes and values of all members of the family – including the mobility of children (see, for example, Hindess 1981; Heath 1981; Beck

1983). In addition, the income from a wife's employment may mean that *non*-mobile men still have a feeling of advancement in terms of improved living standards. Finally, female mobility is itself relevant to understanding class formation – married women who are *intragenerationally* mobile may have just as much influence on the attitudes and values of the household as their non-mobile husbands. To assume that women's social mobility is not of any relevance to the key questions included in mobility studies would seem naïve as well as sexist.

One must none the less recognize the serious problems entailed in incorporating women into the social mobility studies. Not all married women are in employment, and even where they are this may be part-time, low-status work, taken to fit in with having a family, which would be a poor indicator of their life-style. Also, because married women typically move in and out of the labour market as the demands of their families change, they tend not to have a career in the sense in which at least some men have one (Dex 1984). Furthermore, labour market segmentation means not only that women tend to be concentrated in a narrow range of occupations, but also that the 'class' distribution of women's jobs is different from that of men's; women are concentrated in routine non-manual and unskilled manual occupations and are under-represented in high status occupations and in skilled manual work. Even within occupational classes women often occupy the lower levels and do not reach the higher positions. Nevertheless the majority of women work for the majority of their employable lives (Martin and Roberts 1984).

These technical problems should not be underrated. Conventionally, mobility is measured from father to son (or son-in-law); if we try to include mothers we again face the problem of full-time housewives or women in part-time work. Nevertheless, the intergenerational mobility of women can be of interest and add to our knowledge of mobility patterns. First, it is possible to look at unmarried women and see if their mobility patterns from father to daughter parallel men's mobility from father to son. (This could provide valuable information about gender inequalities as well.) Second, we could look, as some recent studies have, at women's first entry to the job market, and examine how class background and educational achievement influence the status of first jobs. Third, we could examine the occupational class of married women when they *return* to full-time work after completing their families and see how this relates to class background. From this kind of analysis it is possible to examine how open British society is for women as compared with men, the extent to which high-status fathers are able to promote their daughters as compared with their sons, and so on.

The patterns of *intra*generational mobility for women are also of considerable interest. Again the mobility patterns for single women can be compared directly with those of men and provide valuable information on gender inequalities. Also, information on the intragenerational mobility of women would give us information on married women's participation in the labour market and movement between non-employment, part-time, and full-time work, as well as women's commitment to paid employment.

Ideally, because of the effect of child-bearing and child-rearing on careers, one needs a longitudinal perspective for examining female social mobility, and one good recent study of this kind (Martin and Roberts 1984) will be cited at relevant points below. However, most mobility studies use cross-sectional data – respondent's occupation now compared with father's highest employment, current employment, or employment at a given age of the respondent. Data on own occupational history are collected retrospectively and are subject to all the usual distortions of memory. The People in Society Survey is no exception, nor was it developed specifically to examine social mobility. However, information is available on own, husband's, and father's occupation (though not on mother's), as well as on educational qualifications obtained and age on leaving school. (We have in fact recorded the last of these into a measure of years of *post-compulsory* schooling, which is a better indicator – see Abbott 1987.) In order to begin to examine women's social mobility we analyse the intergenerational mobility of different groups of women separately, distinguishing the single from the married, those in full-time employment from part-time workers, and looking at age cohorts separately.

The rest of this chapter, then, examines patterns of female social mobility and compares them with those for men. *Inter*generational mobility will be examined first, in comparison with the most recent British study, the Oxford Mobility study, and then *intra*generational mobility. As well as presenting an analysis of our own data we shall summarize the findings from American and British studies of female social mobility. Our own data not only provide material on women's patterns of social mobility but also give the reader information on the women whose images of class are the focus of attention in the remainder of the book. They tell us where they have come from in class terms, their own current occupational class, and the class of the men to whom they are married.

The reader should be warned that comparison of different mobility studies is something to be undertaken with caution, because of the different ways in which studies categorize occupation. The People in Society Survey uses the Social Grading Scheme (see Chapter 2), but it is unique among mobility studies in doing so. Glass *et al.* (1954), for example, used the Hall-Jones seven-point scale, and this in turn is not strictly comparable with the Hope-Goldthorpe Scale used by the Oxford Study or the modified form of it used in the Scottish Mobility Study. One may question even whether classes *do* form a vertically ordered hierarchy. It is generally assumed that mobility studies measure movement up or down a ladder of hierarchically organized classes/status categories – see, for example, Kelsall, Kelsall, and Chisolm (1984) – and this is certainly the case for most of the American studies, as well as for Glass *et al.* (1954). However, Goldthorpe *et al.* (1980), while placing clerical workers, foremen, shopkeepers, and skilled manual workers in four distinct classes, argue that they are at the same level and that it is therefore not appropriate to talk about vertical mobility between these classes. Conversely, other mobility studies have been concerned with movement between these very groups – that is, with movement between non-manual (middle class) and manual (working class) – see, for example, Lipset and Bendix (1959), Glass *et al.* (1954). Blau and Duncan (1967) are more interested in movement up and down an occupational struc-ture which is conceived as more or less continuous rather than as made up of distinct classes. Indeed, American studies following Blau and Duncan frequently talk about occupational or status mobility rather than class mobility. That is, occupation is used as an indicator of prestige or socio-economic status rather than of class position, and the investigators could be said to be measuring prestige mobility.

In practice, as Heath (1981) points out, most of the classifications of social class/status are broadly similar, whatever their theoretical underpinnings, though they may differ in points of detail. There is a general consensus on which occupations are to be found at the extremes of the distribution – that is, higher administrative and professional jobs in the highest category and semi- and unskilled manual labour in the lowest. Disagreement tends to be concentrated in the middle, around the non-manual/manual divide, and whether classes in the middle of the distribution can be located hierarchically in relation to each other. Thus providing caution is exercised valid comparison may none the less be made. (Some idea of the extent to which the various scales are roughly comparable is given in Chapter 2.)

Intergenerational marital mobility

Conventionally, a woman's class is determined by the occupation of the head of household. For married women this is almost always the occupation of her husband, while her class of origin is determined by the occupation of her father. A married woman's intergenerational mobility is thus determined by comparing the occupations of two men. Even so measured, her mobility is of some potential interest to conventional class theory. It is an additional measure of the fluidity of the class structure – the extent of upward and downward mobility and the extent to which 'privileged' fathers are able to secure the future of their daughters as well as their sons. Also, it is important in understanding class formation; a married woman's class background will have influenced her attitudes and values and these in turn may well influence her husband and children. Thus where the class background of the wife is different from that of her husband it could well be a factor in the intragenerational mobility of her husband and the intergenerational mobility of her children, as well as influencing the political attitudes of the household. Also of relevance is the continuation of kinship ties that cut across classes (see e.g. Goldthorpe *et al.* 1969; Jackson and Marsden 1966; Heath 1981). Putting it another way, a husband's marital mobility is of just as much interest as the marital mobility of his wife.

Studies in the United States, where research on female mobility has been carried out more systematically, have suggested that there is considerable female mobility via marriage, although there is some disagreement as to exactly what the patterns are. Some studies have suggested that intergenerational mobility through marriage for women is very similar in degree and extent to intergenerational occupational mobility for men (Tyre and Treas 1974; Rosenfeld 1978). Glenn *et al.* (1974) argue that women are more likely to be *downwardly* mobile through marriage than men are through occupation and that they are *much* more likely to be downwardly mobile across the manual/non-manual divide. On the other hand, Chase (1975) suggests that women have greater mobility both upwards *and* downwards through marriage than men do through occupation and that women are more likely to cross the boundary between blue and white collar by this means in either direction. He argues further than sons are much more likely to inherit the status of their fathers and that there is thus a greater association between the status positions of fathers and sons than fathers and daughters (i.e. sons-in-law). However, he accepts that the differences between women's intergenerational mobility through marriage and men's through occupation are small when compared to those between men's and women's intergenerational occupational mobility.

Heath (1981) looked at the marital mobility of the wives of the male sample in the Oxford Mobility Study; he compared the occupation of father-in-law when the wife was fourteen with the occupation of son-in-law. He found no large-scale tendency for women to 'marry up', but did find a slight tendency for high-status women not to marry (possibly to avoid 'marrying down') and some evidence that 'low origin' men may be at a slight disadvantage in the marriage market. There was more fluidity in female marriage mobility than male intergenerational mobility – a good deal of 'marrying up' was counterbalanced by an equal incidence of 'marrying down'. The Scottish Mobility Study found that 42.3 per cent of women 'married up', 23.6 per cent married within the occupational class of their fathers, and 36.7 per cent 'married down'. (These figures may be compared with male intergenerational occupational mobility of 42.4 per cent up, 27.4 static and 30.4 down.) As with the US studies, the analysis of female marital mobility suggests perhaps a little more fluidity in the class system than father-son mobility would suggest. However, it is important to note that the differences are far from large and may, as Goldthorpe and Payne (1986) point out in their analysis of 1983 British General Election Survey data, be the 'outcome of various different processes of class reproduction and exchange of a limited and perhaps contradictory kind' (p. 539).

The People in Society Survey also suggests considerable female marital mobility (see *Tables 10–12*). *Table 11* compares occupation of father-in-law with that of son-in-law. Looking first at women from professional and managerial backgrounds (categories A and B), we can see that a large majority married husbands in similar occupations to their fathers. Seventy-eight per cent of the daughters of higher professional and managerial men married either men in the same class (33 per cent) or men in semi-professional and lower managerial jobs (45 per cent). Similarly, the daughters of semi-professional and lower managerial men either married men in the higher professional class (21 per cent) or in the same class (52 per cent). Conversely, only

Table 10   Married women in the survey: Class of husband and father

| class of father | class of husband | | | | | |
| | A | B | C1 | C2 | D | total |
			% table total			
A	3.4	4.7	0.7	1.4	<0.1	10.3
B	4.0	10.2	2.5	2.0	0.7	19.4
C1	1.8	6.0	3.7	4.5	2.2	18.3
C2	1.7	9.0	4.5	17.5	4.3	37.0
D	0.6	2.1	1.5	6.7	4.2	15.1
TOTAL	11.6	31.9	13.0	32.0	11.4	100
estimated % in the population						
A	2.4	4.6	0.8	2.2	0.2	
B	2.6	9.3	2.8	2.9	1.8	
C1	0.9	4.3	3.3	5.2	4.5	
C2	0.8	5.9	3.6	18.6	8.0	
D	0.2	1.2	1.0	6.0	6.6	

N = 1,495   120 cases excluded from the table: missing values or classified E on one or both variables.

Table 11 Marital mobility of married women in the sample, by class of origin

class of father	total		class of husband A	B	C1	C2	D
A	154	%	33	45	7	14	1
B	290	%	21	52	13	10	3
C1	273	%	10	33	21	25	12
C2	553	%	5	24	12	47	12
D	225	%	4	14	10	44	28
TOTAL	1,495	%	12	32	13	32	11
estimated % in the population							
A		%	23	44	8	22	3
B		%	14	48	15	15	8
C1		%	5	24	18	29	24
C2		%	2	16	10	50	22
D		%	2	8	9	40	44

Note
120 cases excluded from the table: missing values or classified E on one or both variables.

Table 12 Marital mobility of married women in the sample, by destination class

class of father	class of husband A	B	C1	C2	D	total
TOTAL	173	477	195	479	171	1,495
	%	%	%	%	%	%
A	29	15	6	4	1	10
B	35	32	19	6	6	19
C1	16	19	29	14	19	18
C2	15	28	35	54	37	37
D	5	6	11	21	37	15

Note
120 cases excluded from the table: missing values or classified E on one or both variables

14 per cent of 'A' daughters married C2D men (in manual trades), with only 1 per cent marrying semi- and unskilled men (class D)'. Again with 'B' daughters we find 13 per cent married to C2D men and only 3 per cent to D men. The extremity of the

differences is exaggerated by the unrepresentative distribution of the sample (see Chapter 2), but similar patterns emerge even after correction for the class distribution of women in the population.

If we look at women from semi- and unskilled manual backgrounds we find a somewhat similar position, but with more upward mobility, as would be expected given the changes in occupational structure which have occurred during this century. While only 28 per cent of 'D' daughters have husbands in class D, 72 per cent had husbands in a manual occupation. Again with daughters from a skilled manual background (C2) 47 per cent have a husband who is similarly placed, and over half (59 per cent) have a manual working-class husband. (Correction for unrepresentative sampling in fact increases the size of these figures.) In terms of upward mobility into the A and B strata, 18 per cent of the women from a class D background in the sample made such a move (representing an estimated 10 per cent of the population), and 29 per cent (18 per cent) of women from class C2; however, only 4 per cent of those from a D background and 5 per cent from C2 made the move to class A – that is, achieved long range social mobility by marriage. (As the upper strata are over-represented in the sample, correction reduces both figures to 2 per cent.)

The final occupational status group for examination is C1 – routine non-manual employment. The relative position of this stratum in relation to those above and below it is difficult to determine. While many researchers have argued that this group is middle-class, at least as far as men are concerned (e.g. Lockwood 1958; Crompton and Jones 1984), others have questioned the extent to which it can be seen as a 'higher' class than skilled manual work (Goldthorpe *et al.* 1980). On the other hand, movement between manual and non-manual occupations has generally been seen as of interest in mobility studies. Women with C1 fathers can be seen to have been both upwardly and downwardly mobile on *Table 10*. Only 21 per cent of such daughters in the sample married men in the same stratum; 43 per cent were upwardly mobile (although only 10 per cent 'made it' to class A – representing an estimated 5 per cent in the population), and 37 per cent married manual workers, a majority of these (25 per cent) being skilled manual workers.

Summarizing the amount of mobility between the manual and

non-manual classes overall (from ABC1 to C2D or vice versa), 19.4 per cent of women in the sample were upwardly mobile, 10.9 per cent downwardly mobile, and 69.7 per cent stable. Assessing mobility perhaps more realistically by looking at movement in and out of the semi-professional, professional, and managerial strata, we find that 26 per cent of daughters of manual workers (13.4 per cent of the sample) married into these strata, while 25 per cent of girls born into these strata (7.4 per cent of the sample) married into a lower class.

To conclude, then, while a considerable amount of fluidity is apparent, much of this is short-range, and the pattern seems similar to the male intergenerational occupational mobility found in the Oxford Mobility Study – though there appears to be more downward mobility for women by marriage than for men by occupation. As with the Oxford Mobility Study we find that the majority of the women in the 'A' category come from 'lower' backgrounds (71 per cent), on Table 12. However, a majority (64 per cent) come from AB backgrounds, and only 20 per cent come from manual working-class homes. If we look at the lowest class (the semi- and unskilled manual workers), we find that only 7 per cent of wives come from AB backgrounds, while 74 per cent came from a manual background. The backgrounds of women married to skilled manual workers were no more varied; 75 per cent came from a manual working-class background and only 10 per cent from an AB one. However, while 37 per cent of women married to semi- and unskilled workers had fathers in the same category, only 21 per cent of women married to skilled manual men had fathers in unskilled trades. Fourteen per cent of women married to skilled men had routine non-manual fathers, as did 19

Table 13 Summary table: marital mobility in the People in Society Survey (%)

class of father	class of husband					dichotomized class	
	total	AB	C1	C2	D	middle	working
	%	%	%	%	%	%	%
Same as husband	47.7	51.3	28.5	54.7	36.8	51.2	65.3
Higher	18.3	—	24.6	24.7	63.2	—	34.7
Lower	33.9	48.7	46.9	20.6	—	48.8	—

per cent of the wives of semi- and unskilled men. Women married to routine non-manual men were the only group who can fairly be said to come from a variety of backgrounds (though the majority – 54 per cent – came from a non-manual one). Thirty-five per cent had skilled and 11 per cent semi- or unskilled fathers, while 6 per cent had class A fathers and 19 per cent B fathers. We can see, therefore, that if we compare a woman's class of origin with her class by marriage there is considerable mobility, resulting in a substantial number of cross-class marriages. However, the distance of 'movement' is typically not great. The pattern of mobility in Britain is very similar to that found in the United States.

It would be of considerable interest to examine the exact mechanisms of marital mobility: that is, are women actually mobile on marriage or do they move via their own occupations? In other words, are we measuring mobility from father to son-in-law or is there an important intervening variable, the woman's own occupation prior to marriage? Unfortunately we know of no survey data – including the People in Society Survey – that would enable us to examine this question in any great detail. (*Current* occupation of married women (see Chapter 1) is not a good guide to occupation on marriage. Also we would need information about husbands' jobs at the time of marriage, as there may have been intragenerational mobility since marriage.) What we can do, however, is look at a small sub-sample of the women to see if this provides any hint of what the pattern might be. It is arguable that married women younger than 25 years who are working full-time are in an occupation that is in some way related to their true potential market position – that is, they have probably not yet had a career interrupted by children, nor taken a part-time job to fit in with domestic responsibilities. However, this sub-sample is very small – only 89 women – so any conclusions can at best be only tentative. *Tables 14* and *15* show class of father and class of husband for this sub-sample, and *Table 16* class of husbands and class of wives.

Looking at background first, we find that all the women in this sub-sample married to husbands in class A came from an AB background, but that about half of the wives of class B men came from manual backgrounds. On the other hand, 46 per cent of women from AB backgrounds have husbands in a manual

Table 14 Marital mobility of married women in the sample aged <25 in full-time employment, by class of origin

class of father	total		class of husband				
			A	B	C1	C2	D
AB	26	%	23	27	4	23	23
C1	8	%	—	12	12	50	25
C2	37	%	—	22	14	65	—
D	16	%	—	6	—	44	50
TOTAL	87	%	7	21	8	46	18

Note
Two cases with missing values on one or both variables have been omitted from the table.

Table 15 Marital mobility of married women in the sample aged <25 in full-time employment by destination class

class of father	class of husband					
	A	B	C1	C2	D	total
	%	%	%	%	%	%
AB	100	38	14	15	37	31
C1	—	6	14	10	12	9
C2	—	50	72	58	—	42
D	—	6	—	17	50	18
Numbers in sample	6	18	7	40	16	87

Note
Two cases with missing values on one or both of the variables have been excluded from the table.

Table 16 Married working women aged <25 in full-time employment: husbands categorized by own occupation

husband's occupation	total		own occupation				
			A	B	C1	C2	D
AB	25	%	—	16	72	8	4
C1	7	%	—	—	57	43	—
C2	38	%	—	—	24	45	32
D	18	%	—	—	44	—	56
TOTAL	88	%	—	4	44	25	26

Note
One case excluded from the table: value missing on husband's occupation.

occupation. Similar trends are evident for class D. Fifty per cent of the women married to class D husbands come themselves from a D background, and 50 per cent of women from a D background married husbands in that class; on the other hand, 37 per cent of women married to class D men come from an AB background, and 23 per cent of women with a class AB background are married to class D men. (The size of the sub-sample does not justify generalization to probable distributions in the population as a whole.) *Table 16* shows that these women are overall most likely to have C1 jobs – almost certainly no higher – and that there is some association with husband's job; over half of the women married to men in class D occupations are themselves in class D occupations, and 88 per cent of women married to AB husbands are in B or C1 jobs. Mobility as judged by own (probably pre-marital) job level and husband's would appear considerable but mixed, conditioned by the preponderance of women in C1 jobs and of men in C2 and D ones (at this age) at the expense of C1, which is a rare category for men; what one sees is apparent movement 'down' when such women marry manual workers or up if they marry AB ones.

Intergenerational occupational mobility

There have been few studies comparing father's occupation with daughter's (and even fewer have compared daughter's occupation with mother's). Yet there are a number of reasons, as we have already argued, why an analysis of female mobility in terms of own occupation is essential both for class theory and for understanding sexual stratification. Problems in interpreting the data have already been discussed; not only (as with male mobility) does change in the structure of occupations over time have implications for the assessment of class mobility, but also the concentration of women in a limited number of occupations distorts comparisons.

One of the major factors here is the huge growth in routine non-manual work for women since the Second World War. We need to consider, rather than taking the answer for granted, whether women in such occupations are or are not middle-class – that is, whether moving from a manual background into this kind of work represents upward mobility. Crompton and Jones

(1984) have argued that as the situation stands, routine non-manual work for women cannot be considered as middle-class, because women who do it do not have the same opportunities for advancement as men do. They do suggest, however, that this situation may change. Lewellyn (1981), in a small-scale study, suggests that as far as bank clerical work is concerned women are recruited with lower educational qualifications than men are; from the outset it is assumed that men will advance to the higher positions while women will not. However, Heath and Britten (1984) argue that, with the exception of shop work, women in routine non-manual occupations enjoy conditions of employment comparable with those enjoyed by middle-class men. Martin and Roberts (1984) suggest that full-time female non-manual workers have middle-class conditions of employment, but not part-time ones. In terms of women's own perceptions, Holland (1981) found that girls from manual homes who wanted to obtain routine non-manual positions when they left school regarded skilled manual work as 'the same sort of thing' for boys, and Webb (1985), in an ethnographic study of female workers in a department store, found that women who had been in a trade in the past saw shop work as 'down' on their previous skilled manual work. However, Abbott (1987) found that in terms of subjective social class identification and social imagery C1 women were comparable with C1 men.

The debate goes on, and we cannot hope to settle it here. What we will do is to analyse movement in and out of class AB separately from class C1, so that we can look at what may be seen as unambiguously middle-class as well as the more ambiguous C1 category. We shall also look at single women separately from married ones, those working full-time separately from those working part-time, and pick out sub-samples by age, in an attempt to control for women's movement in and out of the labour force and for the effect that domestic responsibilities have on women's career patterns. One major problem with father/son mobility studies is that of comparing like with like – ensuring that father's and son's occupations are being measured at comparable stages of 'career'. This is even more problematic for women, who may take part-time work to fit in with domestic responsibilities – the status of such work generally not being the same as that of positions they have held in the past or may hold in the future. It seems likely, then, that the class distribution of women as measured by reference to their own occupations will be markedly different, even allowing for gender differences in the occupational structure, from that of men.

Studies in the United States (e.g. Tyre and Treas 1974; Hauser *et al.* 1975) have found that patterns of female and male intergenerational mobility are indeed dissimilar; they tend to conclude that this is mainly because of the patterns of occupational distribution by sex. (The differences, though significant, tend to be small.) Additionally, Hauser *et al.* have argued that when studying female intergenerational mobility it is important to include the mother's occupation. They suggest that this is a significant factor in female labour market commitment and occupational choice, and thus a key predictor of mobility. (Nevertheless we know of no study to date that has included mother's occupation in the analysis for women. Beck (1983) included mother's occupation for men and found it to have a small but significant effect.) However, while Britain and the United States are in many ways similar in their economic system, it is not necessarily the case that female job opportunities and female labour market preferences will be the same. Both countries have a labour market considerably segregated by gender, with women concentrated into a similar narrow range of occupations. The percentage of women reaching top positions is also low in both countries. However, as Dex (1985) points out, the patterns of women's labour market participation are not the same. In the United States child-care payments are tax deductable, which means that fewer women than in Britain leave work on the birth of their children, and American women are more likely than British ones to be in full-time jobs if they are in employment.

Nevertheless, in a comparative study of female and male social mobility in Sweden and Finland, Erikson and Pontinen (1985) found (as the US studies had done) a higher rate of social mobility for women than men. They conclude that the main differences in outflow distribution are between the sexes and not between countries, and that this is a result of sex-segmented labour markets. Thus women are more frequently found in routine non-manual and unskilled occupations, while men are more likely to obtain jobs in the service class and in skilled manual occupations. Women from all origins are more likely than men to end up in routine non-manual occupations, while sons, irrespective of origins, have a clear advantage in job prospects over daughters. The greater relative mobility rate of women is therefore accounted for on the one hand by downward or upward mobility into routine non-manual work or on the other by downward mobility into unskilled manual labour.

The Oxford Mobility Study did not include women in its sample, but there has been one recent British study which *has* examined female intergenerational social mobility. The Scottish Mobility Study, while unable for financial reasons to draw an independent sample of women, did include the wives of their male sample (Chapman 1984). The study was carried out in 1974–5 and closely resembles the Oxford study in design. Five thousand men born between 1909 and 1955 were interviewed, and 3,500 interviews were also carried out with the male respondents' wives. The measure of occupational grading used was the Payne Scale of Occupational Prestige, which is very similar to the Hope-Goldthorpe scale. The analysis of female mobility was concerned with occupational participation and mobility, and not with class formation, consciousness or action (Chapman 1984).

Chapman argues that in Scotland, as in the rest of Great Britain, considerable labour market segmentation means that women are concentrated in certain industries: in service work, and in lower-paid semi-professional and routine non-manual work. Women in manual work tend, as elsewhere, to be classified as semi- or unskilled rather than skilled. However, he is cautious about generalizing his findings to England and Wales; while the occupational structure is broadly similar, there are certain significant differences. For example, there is a higher level of non-manual employment in England and Wales than in Scotland. Comparing male mobility in Scotland with that in England and Wales (Goldthorpe *et al.* 1980), Scottish men were less likely to be upwardly mobile than men in England and Wales, and, if mobile, less likely to achieve professional or managerial occupations. Chapman concludes that the differences in occupational structure between England/Wales and Scotland have an effect on patterns of occupational mobility. It seems likely, then, that female mobility patterns found in Scotland will not be directly generalizable to England and Wales.

In analysing the patterns of female mobility we have to take account of the differences in occupational distribution between the sexes and between countries, as well as changes in overall occupational structure during the period under analysis – 1931–1971 in the case of the Scottish Mobility Study. However, in general the proportion of women in various industrial sectors seems to be more or less similar across time.

In measuring intergenerational mobility the respondent's current occupation was compared with that of the father when the son or daughter was 14 years old. Comparing male with female mobility, it appeared from the results that men were more likely to be upwardly mobile than women. In terms of origins there was considerable similarity between the male and female respondents, but in terms of destination considerable differences. While men were relatively evenly spread across the professional, lower professional and technical/supervisory categories (with 12–14 per cent in each), but with less than 6 per cent in routine non-manual employment, the majority of female non-manual workers were concentrated in the lower professional and routine non-manual categories, with only a tiny number in professional or technical/supervisory employment. Among manual workers the proportion of men in the skilled and semi-skilled categories was much the same, with fewer in the unskilled category; women, however, were concentrated in unskilled and semi-skilled occupations. In fact, the high level of female mobility was accounted for almost entirely by the concentration of women in lower professional, routine non-manual, and semi-skilled manual occupations. At the extremes of the distribution the patterns for men and women were dissimilar; for example, 70 per cent of men with a professional father themselves had a semi-professional or higher occupation, compared with 45 per cent of the daughters of professional men. Women with manual fathers were more likely to be in semi-skilled work than men with the same background, and less likely to achieve a higher professional occupation than men. Chapman (1984) therefore concludes that there is considerable intergenerational mobility for both men and women, but that female mobility is restricted by structural factors and especially the limited availability of professional, supervisory, technical, and skilled manual opportunities for women. These findings are largely confirmed by the Goldthorpe and Payne analysis of the 1983 General Election Survey. There the mobility rates out of Classes I and II were 66 per cent for women compared with 28 per cent for men, and the rates of mobility into Classes I and II were 11 per cent for women and 27 per cent for men.

The People in Society Survey asked female respondents for their own occupation and that of their father. Those who were not currently employed (and had not been employed for the past two years) have been excluded from the analysis. There is no satisfactory way at present, as we argued in Chapter 1, of allocating an occupational class to women who are not in employment, but the survey's compromise of asking for most recent job for those who have been unemployed for less than two years and comparing current or most recent job with father's job at retirement or at the time of the survey seems not a bad compromise. (It might, perhaps, have been better to ask for father's job at some determinate age of the respondent, as in the Oxford and Scottish studies, but this still introduces systematic biases, though of a different kind from those which the survey's procedures introduce.) Data were of course also collected on males in the People in Society Survey, but we have decided to take the Oxford Mobility Survey's data on males as our main basis of comparison with our data on women, as many readers will be familiar with at least the broad outline of its conclusions, because it is one of the British surveys most commonly used as a comparison-base, and because its sample is larger than ours.

In terms of intergenerational mobility, the Oxford study (which was based on a sample of 10,000 men living in England and Wales in 1972 and aged between 20 and 64) demonstrated a considerable amount of upward mobility combined with upper-class stability (see *Tables 17* and *18*). Seventy-two per cent of the sample could be described as mobile, and the significance of the manual/non-manual divide as a boundary to movement seemed to have declined since the Glass *et al.* study in 1954.

Looking at the sons of Class I fathers we can see that nearly 50 per cent achieved class I and a further 19 per cent class II

Table 17   Oxford Mobility Study (men): Occupational mobility by class of origin

father's occupation	total		own occupation						
			I	II	III	IV	V	VI	VII
I	582	%	48.4	18.9	9.3	8.2	4.5	4.5	6.2
II	477	%	31.9	22.6	10.7	8.0	9.2	9.0	8.0
III	594	%	19.2	15.7	10.8	8.6	13.0	15.0	17.8
IV	1,223	%	12.8	11.1	7.8	24.9	8.7	14.7	19.9
V	939	%	15.4	13.2	9.4	8.0	16.6	20.1	17.2
VI	2,312	%	8.4	8.9	8.4	7.1	12.2	29.6	25.4
VII	2,216	%	6.9	7.8	7.9	6.8	12.5	23.5	34.8
TOTAL	8,343	%	14.3	11.4	8.6	9.9	11.6	20.8	23.3

Table 18   Oxford Mobility Study (men): Occupational mobility by destination class

father's occupation	respondent's occupation							total
	I	II	III	IV	V	VI	VII	
	%	%	%	%	%	%	%	%
I	23.6	11.6	7.5	5.8	2.7	1.5	1.9	7.0
II	12.7	11.4	7.1	4.6	4.5	2.7	2.0	5.7
III	9.5	9.8	8.9	6.1	7.9	5.1	5.5	7.1
IV	13.1	14.3	13.3	36.7	10.9	10.4	12.5	14.7
V	12.1	13.1	12.2	9.0	16.1	10.9	8.3	11.3
VI	16.3	21.6	26.9	19.6	29.2	39.4	30.2	27.7
VII	12.7	18.1	24.1	18.1	28.6	30.0	39.7	26.6
Numbers in sample	1,197	948	721	830	969	1,734	1,944	8,343

occupations. Of the *c.* 24 per cent who were downwardly mobile out of classes I and II only about 11 per cent ended up in manual occupations. Conversely, if we look at the destination of sons with semi- or unskilled manual fathers we find that 65 per cent were upwardly mobile, though only 23 per cent crossed the manual/non-manual divide, and about 15 per cent reached classes I or II. Much of the upward mobility is structural; over three-quarters of the men in class I had lower origins, but 50 per cent of men with class I fathers had ended up in Class I by the time of the survey, so the number of such jobs must have expanded. Looking at men in manual occupations, we find that about 70 per cent of those in skilled manual work had a manual background, as did 70 per cent of those in semi- or unskilled jobs, but only 4 per cent of manual workers came from a class I or class II background. Thus there is considerable heterogeneity in the middle classes and homogeneity in the working class in terms of class origin.

The occupational categories used in the People in Society Survey are not directly comparable with the classification used in the Oxford study. However, categories A, B, and C1 are roughly comparable to classes I, II, and III and D to VII; C2, however, is a broader category than VI and would include most of IV and V on the Hope-Goldthorpe scale.

Looking at intergenerational mobility for *men* in the People in Society Survey, we find a broadly comparable pattern to that revealed by the Oxford study. However, it tends to suggest an even greater ability for high-status fathers to promote their sons than the Oxford study did, and for there to be less upward mobility from the working class to the professional, semi-professional and managerial strata. It also provides less evidence of structural mobility, which might have come about for a number of reasons. The Oxford study looked only at men living in England and Wales, while the People in Society Survey also covers Scotland and Northern Ireland. (The Scottish Mobility Study showed less upward mobility than the Oxford one – see Chapman 1984.) The Oxford study was carried out in 1972, while our data come from the period 1980–1984; there have been increases in unemployment between 1972 and 1984, and in the numbers of men taking early retirement. On the other hand, the Oxford study used a stratified random sample rather than the quota methods of the People in Society Survey and is thus more likely to be representative of the population. Finally, the different social class categorizations used in the two studies makes precise comparison difficult. We suspect that all these factors are relevant in explaining the discrepancies.

The Inflow and Outflow tables for social mobility of all women in the People in Society Survey sample are given as *Table 19* and *20* (the full mobility table is *Table 23*). Comparing *Table 19* with *Table 17*, we see a very different picture. Only 8 per cent of the daughters of men in professional and managerial occupations (as compared with nearly 50 per cent of sons in the Oxford Mobility Study)

Table 19   Employed women in the sample: Occupational mobility by class of origin

father's occupation	numbers in sample		own occupation A	B	C1	C2	D
A	200	%	8	38	44	6	4
B	354	%	2	41	44	8	5
C1	310	%	2	24	46	10	19
C2	693	%	<1	14	32	19	35
D	253	%	<1	12	27	13	48
TOTAL	1,810	%	2	23	37	13	25
estimated % in the population							
A		%	5	38	49	4	4
B		%	1	40	48	5	6
C1		%	1	23	49	6	20
C2		%	<1	14	35	12	39
D		%	<1	11	29	8	51

Note
134 cases excluded from the table: missing values or coded E on one or both of the variables.

Table 20   Employed women in the sample: Occupational mobility by destination class

father's occupation	own occupation A	B	C1	C2	D	total
	%	%	%	%	%	%
A	50	17	13	5	2	11
B	24	35	23	12	4	20
C1	15	17	21	13	13	17
C2	9	23	33	56	54	38
D	3	7	10	14	27	14
Numbers in sample	34	420	674	232	450	1,810

Note
134 cases excluded from the Table: missing values or coded E on one or both variables.

have *not* been downwardly mobile. (However, only 10 per cent have been downwardly mobile into the manual working class.) Conversely, 48 per cent of the daughters of semi- or unskilled men have *not* been mobile (compared with about 35 per cent of men in the Oxford study); while less than 1 per cent have achieved professional or managerial status, 12 per cent have reached semi-professional or lower managerial employment, and in total 39 per cent have crossed the manual/non-manual divide. Forty-four per cent of the women in the sample were upwardly mobile from the manual to the non-manual strata, although 31 per cent ended up in routine non-manual jobs. Fifty-six per cent of the women were downwardly mobile from classes A or B, but only 12 per cent crossed over into a manual occupation, 44 per cent ending up in routine non-manual work. We can conclude that there is considerable female intergene-rational mobility, as indicated by own employment, that down-ward mobility occurs more frequently for women than for men, and that women of whatever origin are more likely than men to end up in routine non-manual jobs. Indeed, the vast majority of the women who cross the manual/non-manual divide end up in this category. While the manual/non-manual divide appears to act as a barrier to downward mobility, upward mobility through the divide is more frequent. (The effect of correcting for unrepresentative sampling is to increase the amount of downward mobility from Classes A and B and of upward mobility from C2 and D, both going to increase the C1 figures.)

Looking at *Table 20*, we see that, as for men, a considerable amount of apparent mobility is structural in origin, and that while the middle classes are heterogeneous (though not as much so as the men in the Oxford study), the manual strata tend towards homogeneity. Twenty-seven per cent of semi- and unskilled female manual workers came from that background, and 81 per cent from a manual working-class background. Similarly, 56 per cent of C2 daughters had C2 fathers, and 70 per cent had working-class fathers. Conversely, only 6 per cent of those in semi- or unskilled manual employment came from classes A or B, and only 17 per cent of those in skilled manual occupations. Of the small number who were in professional or managerial occupations, 50 per cent came from a similar background and 12 per cent from manual working-class back-grounds. However, we find greater heterogeneity if we look at class B, the semi-professional and lower managerial group: while 52 per cent of the women in this stratum did come from

Table 21   Employed women in the sample: Own and father's occupation

father's occupation	A	B	C1	C2	D	total
			own occupation			
			% table total			
A	0.9	4.1	4.8	0.7	0.5	11.0
B	0.4	8.0	8.5	1.6	1.0	19.6
C1	0.3	4.0	8.0	1.6	3.2	17.1
C2	0.2	5.4	12.2	7.2	13.4	38.3
D	0.1	1.7	3.8	1.8	6.7	14.0
TOTAL	1.9	23.2	37.2	12.8	24.9	100

Note
N = 1,810

the same or a higher group, 30 per cent came from a manual working-class background.

However, these data are based on all the working women in the sample. The data as presented substantiate the argument that female employment patterns differ considerably from male ones and that women are distributed differently from men in the hierarchy of occupations; this clearly affects patterns of female intergenerational mobility (at least when measured from father to daughter). One of the problems in looking at all the women together, however, is that some of those included are in part-time work which may be of low status and taken to fit in with family commitments. We checked this by looking separately at women in full-time and part-time employment, and within these broad groups at married and single women separately. We found very similar patterns across all groups, which seems to indicate that gender rather than marital status or even being in part-time employment seems to be the key factor in labour market segmentation, and that this is the key factor in determining the patterns of female intergenerational mobility. Our conclusions are broadly comparable with those of Chapman's 1984 analysis of the data on women from the Scottish Mobility Study. We must conclude, therefore, that women's social mobility is considerably influenced by their gender and that this factor must be seen as a key one when analysing the openness of British society. Class background and gender interact to determine the mobility patterns of people living in contemporary Britain. Furthermore, this is as true for men as women.

At this point in the analysis it would be usual in discussions of social mobility to introduce a correction for changes in the occupational structure over time, in order to eliminate by statistical means that part of apparent social mobility which is due entirely to growth or decline in a type of occupation. Clearly if there are more middle-class jobs now then were available in our fathers' time – which there are – then a greater proportion of the current population *must* be in the middle class, and therefore some apparent mobility will have been created. Chapman (1984) demonstrates that when this factor is controlled in studies of male intergenerational mobility, the level of upward mobility declines quite markedly. He also demonstrates, however (see Chapman 1984: 170–73) that there is no practical way of applying such a correction when comparing father's job with *daughter's*, because of the different distribution of occupations by gender. Correction by comparison of *mother's* and daughter's job is also unsound, because fewer married women took paid employment in the earlier generation and because of women's interrupted job patterns. Relative and absolute rates of mobility can still be analysed provided caution is taken, as Chapman points out, but we cannot eliminate the spurious effects of historical changes in occupational structure by a simple statistical manipulation, as would be possible for men. (This raises an interesting point: given changing numbers of women in paid employment, and changing patterns of occupational segregation by gender, a further portion of apparent male mobility may in fact be spurious, being due entirely to the 'invasion' of certain levels of occupation by female labour, 'driving' men into higher strata. We discuss this in Chapter 7.)

Class origins and gender are not, of course, the only determinants of women's occupational position. A woman's class destination is not fixed at birth – there is a considerable amount of intergenerational mobility, and women are found in all classes, albeit differently distributed from men. In a causal path analysis of the Oxford data, with occupational distribution as the ultimate dependent variable (reported by Heath 1981), the residual (unknown) factors actually came up for men as the largest 'explanatory' term, substantially larger than any of the explanatory factors included in the analysis (father's education, father's occupation, own education, own first job, present job). Own education came up as the most important of the variables included, however – influenced in its turn by father's job and father's education, but there was substantial variation in the educational achievement of men from the same social background. It would seem likely that this variable would be at least as important for women as for men.

Jones (1986) looked at social mobility among 16–29 year olds (men, and women without children), using General Household Survey data for 1979 and 1980 and National Child Development Survey data, and considered the importance of educational qualifications and class origins in determining the status of first job. She found that class of origin and level of educational qualification were important factors for both boys and girls, though she points out that for women the effect is more difficult to see because of the heavy concentration of women in routine non-manual jobs. For example, she found that 86 per cent of the daughters of manual workers who stayed on in education past the age of 18 had non-manual first jobs, compared with 63 per cent of those who left early. On the other hand 76 per cent of those who left early among the daughters of non-manual men were in non-manual employment.

The People in Society Survey results suggest a strong relationship between education and occupational class. *Table 22*

Table 22 Own occupation, father's occupation, and percentage of women with 2 or more years of post-compulsory education

father's occupation	A	B	own occupation C1	C2	D	total
A	82	78	68	57	33	12
B	86	84	68	43	11	72
C1	100	78	49	50	3	52
C2	100	81	37	7	8	34
D	100	90	55	—	—	32
TOTAL	86	82	53	18	5	N=1,417

Note
450 cases excluded from the table — missing values or coded E on an occupation variable.

shows the relationship between father's occupational class, own occupational class, and whether the respondents stayed on at school beyond the statutory minimum school leaving age. We can see that, irrespective of class background, those in AB jobs had generally stayed on two years or more, and only a small proportion had left at the first opportunity. For women in C1 jobs a different picture emerges – only half stayed on at school for two or more years. Skilled manual women show a similar pattern; those from non-manual homes were as likely to have stayed on at school as to have been early leavers, while those from manual homes generally left school early. Of the women in semi– or unskilled jobs, however, the vast majority were early leavers, with the exception of women from a professional or managerial background. This analysis looks at all working women, and we have already cast doubt on the practice of using present job as a valid indicator of married women's potential occupational class, especially if the current job is a part-time one. Numbers would be too small in each cell if we attempted to look at different groups of women separately. However, the overall analysis does suggest a strong relationship between education and present class – women in high-status jobs have generally spent longer in the educational system, irrespective of class of origin.

Table 23 looks at educational qualifications (excluding the 'other' category) and own and father's occupational class. Again we can see that education is an important factor in obtaining high-status occupations. While having educational qualifications does not protect a woman from being in a low-status occupation, the percentage of women with qualifications in the low categories – manual and routine non-manual jobs – is low.

Intragenerational mobility

Another important aspect of mobility is *intra*generational movement, the extent to which an individual moves during his or her own lifetime up or down the class/occupational prestige hierarchy. What determines an individual's movements is also of interest – class background, educational qualifications or 'on the job' factors? In the case of women we would also be interested in the ways in which marriage, domestic responsibilities, and

Table 23 Own and father's occupation and median level of educational qualification of the employed women in the sample

father's occupation			own occupation			
	A	B	C1	C2	D	total
A	5	5	3	2	2	5
B	3	5	3	2	2	4
C1	—	5	3	2	1	3
C2	5	5	2	2	1	4
D	5	5	4	2	1	4
TOTAL	5	5	3	2	1	N=1,269

Notes
The educational levels are coded as follows:
1 none   4 HNC/teacher's certificate
2 CSE/'O' level   5 degree or equivalent
3 'A' level/ONC
598 cases excluded from the table – missing values, coded E on an occupational variable, or educational qualification recorded as 'other'.

childbirth or child-rearing influence women's occupational mobility – especially when this involves movement into or out of an occupational class. Given women's domestic responsibilities and the fact that women tend not to have a continuous relationship to the labour market, we would expect women to experience less upward intragenerational mobility than men. One British study (Harris and Clausen 1967) did indeed find that women experienced less overall mobility than men; most of the mobility that did occur was downward from skilled manual work.

The more recent Oxford Mobility Study, in its male sample, found a considerable amount of intragenerational mobility. Fifty per cent of men in Classes 1 and 2 who emerged as *intergener-ationally* stable had been downwardly mobile in the interim; that is, they had started from occupations lower down the class scale and had been intragenerationally mobile back to their fathers' level. Of the men from working-class homes, 75 per cent initially had working-class jobs, but by 1972 only half of these were still in manual occupations. Goldthorpe *et al.* (1980) conclude that there is considerable intragenerational mobility but that once the higher classes have been reached the individual tends to stay there for the rest of his working life. In other words, much of this apparent intragenerational mobility may be explained as normal career progression involving a start at a level below the father's and the eventual achievement of the father's level through career advancement. Also, mobility was of most frequent occurrence in the intermediate groups (III, IV, and V), and while there was no clear pattern to the movement, movement between these classes was not seen as significant except in as much as they provided stepping stones up or down.

The Scottish Mobility Study (Chapman 1984) found that on entry to the labour market 75 per cent of men and 77 per cent of women experienced downward mobility. However, men tended to recover their position after a number of years in the labour market. For example, of the sons of semi-professional and professional men who were downwardly mobile to the working class on entry to the labour market, nearly 40 per cent eventually achieved professional status, while of similarly mobile daughters only 12 per cent achieved professional or semi-professional status. In the intermediate strata, 70 per cent of men and 72 per cent of women were downwardly mobile on entry to the labour market. In the case of men a large percentage eventually achieved professional or semi-professional status, though a similar precentage were still in manual jobs at the time of the survey. However, in the case of women only 15 per cent eventually achieved professional or semi-professional status, while 60 per cent remained in manual occupations. A similar picture emerged for manual workers: 65 per cent of sons and 75 per cent of daughters remained in manual work, but of the upwardly mobile nearly twice as many men as women eventually achieved professional or semi-professional status. The major conclusion of the Scottish Mobility Study is that men experience more upward intragenerational mobility than women, and that men are more likely to be countermobile than women.

Jones (1986), using the National Child Development Study data, concludes that women experience more intragenerational stability than men in their careers up to the age of 23. She suggests that intragenerational mobility among young female workers, both up and down, is less common than among young men. Given that education is an important determinant of first occupation, she suggests that for many women their class destination is determined by their education. She then demonstrates that in fact educational qualification is an important factor in female countermobility. Thirteen per cent of middle-class daughters are countermobile: that is, on entry to the labour market they have a manual job but achieve a middle-class one through occupational mobility. Of this 13 per cent, 8 per cent had, in fact, been educated beyond the age of eighteen. (One might therefore raise a question about whether their recorded 'first job' does indeed constitute their real entry to the labour market or whether what was recorded was a holiday job or a part-time job undertaken during schooling or while at college or university.) This compares with 19 per cent of countermobile middle-class sons, 8 per cent of whom reached middle-class occupation via education and work routes, and 11 per cent by work routes alone.

Greenhalgh and Stewart's study (1982) found that men experienced more upward mobility than women and achieved higher occupational status. However, they also found that full-time employed single women experienced less disadvantage than did married or divorced women, and those working full-time 'lost' less than part-time workers.

These studies suggest that women's intragenerational mobility is very limited. However, a more complex picture comes out of the most detailed study to date of women's lifetime work histories, by Martin and Roberts (1984). Their results are based on interviews with 5,588 women of working age in Great Britain in 1980. Of the women in their sample 60 per cent were in paid employment (of whom 56 per cent were working full-time and 44 per cent part-time), 5 per cent described themselves as unemployed, 5 per cent were students, and the remaining 30 per cent were classified as economically inactive. (In 1980 women constituted *c.* 40 per cent of the total workforce.) In terms of labour market participation, their finding is that marriage as such does not affect participation and that 65 per cent of married women are economically active. What does affect participation is having children; women with young children are the most likely to withdraw from the labour force, and only 4 per cent of women continue in employment when they first have a child. None the less the majority of women are economically active for the majority of their employable years –

the older women in the sample had spent 60 per cent of their employable years in employment, and the indications were that the proportion would eventually be greater for the younger women, as they tended to return to work sooner after having a child than was usual in the past. One should note, however, that part-time work is an important facet of women's labour market participation, especially for those who have dependent children, and this is likely to continue given the current restructuring of the labour maket (see Beechey 1984).

Martin and Roberts found that childless women were more likely than women with small children to be in non-manual occupations, and that older childless women were much more likely to be found in the professional and semi-professional categories. Childless women were also more likely to experience upward social mobility than women with children. Of the childless women younger than 30, 12 per cent were in a higher occupational category than when they started work, and the proportion grew to 31 per cent for those aged over 30. During the childless phase of their lives 20 per cent of women now with children had been upwardly intragenerationally mobile before the birth of their first child. The data suggest that in the absence of children women do experience quite high levels of upward social mobility – but still not as high as those experienced by men.

The interesting question is what happens to the women who leave the labour market to have children. Fifty-one per cent of women move class on returning to work after having their children; of these, 37 per cent move down and 14 per cent move up. Those who return to part-time work are more likely to be downwardly mobile than those who take full-time employment – 45 per cent compared with 19 per cent; the full-timers are slightly more likely to be upwardly mobile – 17 per cent, compared with 13 per cent. However, there is some evidence that once women re-enter the labour force there is some upward mobility. Sixty per cent of women who return to work stay in the class at which they re-enter; however, 23 per cent are upwardly mobile and 17 per cent downwardly mobile. Movement from full- to part-time work or vice versa is an important factor in mobility: women who move from part- to full-time work are likely to move up, while those who move from full- to part-time work are more likely to move down in occupational class terms. The longer a woman has been in the labour force, the more chance that she will be upwardly mobile. Finally, if we compare the occupational class of the woman's last job before her first child with her present one we find that 21 per cent are in a higher occupation while 38 per cent are in a lower one. Thus while there is some evidence for recovery over time, interruption of work history and taking part-time employment still remain important factors in explaining female intragenerational mobility. Women's domestic responsibilities seem to be a vital factor in understanding the patterns of intragenerational mobility experienced by married women, and especially by those who have children.

As we have already said, the People in Society Survey did not collect the longitudinal data required for an authoritative analysis of women's work-life mobility. However, it is possible to compare full- and part-time working women, and married and non-married women, to see how the occupational class distributions vary. It is also possible to compare age-cohorts of women to gain some idea of how the distribution varies at different stages in the employment life-cycle. We have divided our sample into three cohorts: those under the age of 25 at the time of the survey, those between 25 and 35, and those over 35. We assume that there will be women who are intending to marry among the single women under 25, but that after that age the majority are more likely to be work-orientated, or at least to be no more constrained by domestic commitments (or perceived to be so constrained) than men are generally assumed to be. We also assume that the majority of married women are in the 'family-building' stage between the ages of 25 and 35, and that this is the period when they are most likely to be outside the labour market if they are going to take time out at all. However, it is difficult to sustain the last point from our data, as analysis is complicated by movements in marital status from single to married as well as by movement in or out of the labour force.

If we look at *Table 24* we can see that the number of women in employment actually increases by age, and that this appears to be true for married but not for single women. The overall distribution by occupational class for all married women is very much as expected – very few women in A or C2 and a large

Table 24 Employed women in the sample: Own occupation by age and marital status

occupation		Age	
	18–24	*25–34*	*35+*
(a) All employed women	%	%	%
A	—	3	2
B	6	32	24
C1	44	34	36
C2	23	10	10
D	27	20	27
Numbers in sample	385	577	867
(b) Married employed women	%	%	%
A	—	1	2
B	5	28	20
C1	50	35	38
C2	24	12	11
D	20	24	29
Numbers in sample	77	374	648
(c) Single employed women	%	%	%
A	—	8	1
B	6	41	54
C1	42	40	34
C2	22	6	3
D	28	5	7
Numbers in sample	308	146	99

concentration in C1 and D. Looking across age cohorts we find a large increase in category B from age <25 to age 25–34 and age 35+. This might suggest more intragenerational mobility than has previously been thought to occur, from routine non-manual to higher grades, and indeed there is a decline in the numbers employed in C1 jobs (but also in C2 jobs), while the number in D remains fairly constant, with a drop in the 25–34 age-group. The same pattern seems to occur (see *Table 25*) if we examine just the women working full-time. However, we see a rather different pattern if we look at just the women working part-time: again

Table 25　Employed women in the sample: Own occupation by age and employment status (%)

occupation		Age	
	18–24	*25–34*	*35+*
(a) *Full-time occupation*	%	%	%
A	—	3	3
B	6	41	35
C1	49	37	34
C2	24	10	8
D	21	9	20
Numbers in sample	336	399	530
(b) *Part-time occupation*	%	%	%
A	—	1	1
B	2	14	7
C1	14	28	40
C2	16	11	13
D	67	46	39
Numbers in sample	49	174	343

there is an increase in the percentage working in B occupations, but there is also a large increase in the C1s and a decline in those in class D.

The majority of part-time female workers are, of course, married, so is it marriage or part-time work that correlates with the changes in class distribution? *Table 26* shows the class distribution for married and for single women in full-time employment. The distributional and cohort changes for married women are comparable to those for full-time working women as a whole. However, we see a slightly different picture when we look at the single women separately: the increase in category B is larger – though the major changes occur between the <25 group and those aged 25–34. This suggests that as women leave the 'single' category on marriage, those who remain have a different occupational class distribution from those who leave. This distribution is still not the same as the male one – single women are heavily concentrated in routine non-manual and semi-professional work, but there is a larger proportion in the former than in the latter. This suggests in turn that some women who

Table 26 Full-time employed women in the sample: Own
occupation by age and marital status (%)

occupation		Age	
	18–24	*25–34*	*35+*
(a) Married women	%	%	%
A	—	1	3
B	6	37	33
C1	58	39	35
C2	20	12	9
D	16	11	21
Numbers in sample	64	220	331
(b) Single women	%	%	%
A	—	9	1
B	6	45	60
C1	47	36	31
C2	25	6	3
D	22	4	6
Numbers in sample	271	138	107

remain single do achieve upward intragenerational mobility, but
that the extent of this is limited and that few women in this
category achieve full professional status.

Finally, looking at married part-time workers (*Table 27*) we
again see a very different class distribution from that of married
full-time workers. The married part-time workers are heavily
concentrated in manual occupations, and for the 25–34 and 35+
cohorts in semi- and unskilled manual work and routine non-
manual work. (The numbers in the <25 cohort are too small to
form the basis of reliable conclusions.)

This analysis suggests that in terms of female intragenerational mobility there is some upward female mobility over time from
C1 to B and that the number of women employed in skilled
manual occupations declines. However, while single women
seem to experience some intragenerational mobility, those in
part-time employment are more likely if anything to be downwardly mobile. There is some evidence also for limited rates of
upward mobility for married women working full-time. However, mobility is limited for all women by the structure of female

Table 27   Married women in part-time employment: Occupation and age

occupation		Age	
	18–24	*25–34*	*35+*
	%	%	%
A	—	1	1
B	—	15	5
C1	—	29	42
C2	50	12	13
D	50	44	39
Numbers in sample	10	147	290

employment. Few women achieve professional or managerial positions, compared with men, and the proportion of women in skilled manual work actually declines over time. While marriage does seem to be one factor limiting women's careers, the more important factor appears to be the adoption of part-time work, once we control for being a women at all. Women, then, seem to be disadvantaged in terms of obtaining high-status occupation in comparison with men whether or not they marry, although having children and taking up part-time work does seem to be a significant factor in downward mobility or lack of advancement.

Finally it must be pointed out that all studies of intragenerational mobility only measure movement between categories, not within them. Women in semi-professional occupations (nurses, teachers, social workers, and so on) could well experience career advancement without moving into a higher occupational stratum. However, the available evidence, in fact, suggests that women are heavily concentrated at the lower end of the career hierarchy in many semi-professional occupations – in other words, men are more likely to be promoted than women – and this appears to be true even in the female-dominated occupations.

Conclusions

An analysis of female social mobility suggests that there is considerable fluidity in the occupational class system. Women are both upwardly and downwardly mobile, both in terms of

marital mobility and in terms of their own occupational placement. As with male mobility, education can be seen to be an
important factor in mobility, and in the case of women
especially upward mobility. However, because of the distribution of female jobs between the occupational categories,
women are more likely to be downwardly mobile than men and
less likely to be upwardly mobile. High-status fathers are less
able to secure high-status occupations for their daughters than
for their sons, and daughters are less likely to be countermobile.
However, the large concentration of women in routine non-
manual work has a significant impact on female social mobility.
While the non-manual/manual divide acts as a barrier to
downward mobility, there is considerable *upward* mobility
across the divide – but most of the upwardly mobile finish up in
routine non-manual work. Furthermore, this pattern of female
intergenerational mobility seems to be a feature of all advanced
industrial societies.

In terms of intragenerational mobility the patterns are complex. Women's domestic responsibilities, especially caring for
children under the age of sixteen, seem to have a marked effect,
and if women returning to the labour market take part-time
work there is a strong likelihood that they will be downwardly
mobile. However, even when single women are examined
separately we find that they experience less intragenerational
mobility than men. Both American and British studies suggest
that educational factors are more important for women than for
men in determining their occupational class irrespective of how
long they have been in the labour market.

These findings suggest that an analysis of male occupational
class mobility by itself is inadequate: such analysis provides a
distorted picture of what is going on, because the experiences of
women are different from those of men and these differences
are not entirely accounted for by women's domestic responsibilities. Class interacts with gender, and the evidence suggests
that men are advantaged because they are men and women
disadvantaged because they are women, in terms of both
*inter*generational and *intra*generational mobility.

However, it is also important to remember that while women
have this in common, class inequalities also divide them. As
Goldthorpe and Payne (1986) argue on the basis of their analysis

of the 1983 General Election Survey, and as our data have shown, there is no evidence to sustain the view that women of all origins share in a common class fate. Women of all origins are not equally likely to end up in the same class; daughters from the top classes are no less likely relative to other women to end up in jobs in those classes than men are relative to other men. If we look at marital mobility we find that high-class fathers are as able to 'protect' the class of their daughters through marriage as they are that of their sons in the labour market. Furthermore, we would agree that studies that incorporate female mobility as well as male mobility do not show markedly different relative mobility rates from studies including only males in the sample. We also have no quarrel with their conclusion that the class distribution of women is a result of the segregated labour market which disadvantages women, and that this accounts for women's high rates of downward mobility. Nor would we question their conclusion that these trends have been ably demonstrated outside of mobility studies.

This does not mean, however, that there is no need to incorporate women in mobility studies; on the contrary, their inclusion is vital for the proper testing of mainstream theory. At the beginning of the chapter we pointed out that Goldthorpe *et al.* (1980) had been explicitly concerned to test three theories: 'social closure', 'buffer zone', and 'counterbalance'. On the basis of their findings they rejected all three. They argued that there was no evidence that those in superior positions were able to prevent upward mobility from lower classes (although they did not examine the élite – their top class was relatively large), or that mobility was restricted to short-range movement around the manual/non-manual divide, or that educational qualifications were the major stimulus for upward mobility. In terms of social closure the People in Society findings for women support Goldthorpe to the extent that there *was* long-range mobility and that high-status fathers were not necessarily able to secure high-status occupations for their daughters. However, some evidence has been presented that in the highest occupational categories men are able to operate social closure against women – there are few women in top jobs. In terms of the buffer zone thesis the findings do not support Goldthorpe; for women the manual/non-manual divide does operate as a buffer zone, with considerable mobility around this area, especially upward from the manual strata, but substantially less beyond it. On the basis of this we must ask, as West has (1978: 232), 'how can women workers be "peripheral" if the "underclass" they so neatly occupy is part of the "buffer zone" which ... helps to prevent polarisation of the two major classes?' Finally, in terms of the 'counterbalance' thesis we have seen that educational qualifications seem to be the major factor in female occupational placement. Women are much less likely to experience intra-generational upward mobility – that is, to be promoted on the basis of work experience as opposed to initial qualification.

At the very least these findings need to be taken into account when making statements about the class structure of modern Britain and about the extent and type of social mobility within it. It could well be that women's occupations are less important than men's and that married women's attitudes and values are shaped more by the class of their households (that is, the occupation of their husbands), that work experience for women has little or no influence on their class attitudes, values, and actions or those of their husbands or children. For example, it could be that a 'white-blouse' worker married to a manual worker exhibits *his* attitudes and values and is little influenced by her fellow workers (some of whom will come from 'middle-class' households) or by her superior work position. It could be that women's attitudes are not affected by their own education or by the class background from which they come. These are factors which need to be explored, however, not taken for granted. Little is known about the class awareness of women and what factors shape their class attitudes, because few researchers have thought the topic worth exploring. Thus we agree with Goldthorpe and Payne that it is necessary 'to bring forward systematic evidence in support of the assumption that married women's own employment can be reliably taken as a major determinant of their class identity' (p. 550), while strongly questioning their assumption that studies which have excluded women have not 'seriously limited or distorted our understanding of class mobility' (p. 550). The rest of this book, then, is concerned with these very issues – the extent to which women's employment can be seen as a major determinant of their class identity.

4 Subjective social class

Introduction

In the previous chapter we saw that patterns of female occupational mobility, both intergenerational and intragenerational, are different from those exhibited by men (and that they may have important consequences for the interpretation of male as well as female mobility data). This tells us very little, however, about how women experience and make sense of the social structure, the main 'question' of this book. In the conclusions to the chapter on female mobility in his 1981 book, Heath argued that the distinctive pattern of female mobility may have important consequences that have not yet been determined.

> 'The outcome for class solidarity and class conflict has yet to be studied, but it may well have the effect of increasing the size of the "middle class" with no strong class allegiance and a more calculative orientation to employers, unions and [political] parties. It may well increase the instability and unpredictability of class action and political preference.'
>
> (Heath 1981: 136)

Thus the study of how women experience their location in the class structure is of vital importance for building an understanding of class orientation and class action. It may well be, of course, that their experiences are constituted as an articulation of class experience, *marital* class experience, and experience of gender subordination. This does not reduce the importance of female perceptions, however, nor reduce the importance of taking them into account if we are to develop class theory to the point where it has explanatory relevance for the whole population. To ignore women is not only to be sex-blind; it is to make the bland assumption that their subjective experience of the social structure is the same as that of their fathers and/or husbands. This in itself is an empirical question – do women married to working-class men have the same social imagery as working-class men? To assume that wives' subjective experience will be mainly determined by the occupations of their husbands or fathers and the patterns of consumption these enable them to enjoy is to ignore altogether the possibility that other factors – their own occupation, education, or position as women – may be equally as important as their head of household's occupation, or even more important.

In this chapter and the next two we begin the process of exploring women's subjective experience of class/status, mainly by exploring the extent to which their perceptions of the social structure appear to be related to their own characteristics or to their husbands' occupation and income. (We recognize, of course, that not all women are living with a man and that single women's experience may well differ from that of married women – as indeed may the experience of women who work full-time as opposed to part-time. We have already noted that mobility patterns vary between different groups of women. Consequently our analysis will often be subdivided by marital and employment status.)

Most of the analysis will mirror research previously carried out on men. We have adopted this pattern not for the sake of inter-sex comparison alone, but also because we believe this is the essential first stage in developing class theory to incorporate women; we need to have comparable information on women to that already collected on men as a preliminary to adequate theorization. This is not because we take an empiricist position, but because it is necessary to demonstrate with empirical findings that existing theory is inadequate – that it ignores the distinctive experiences of women or makes an assumption of similarity to male patterns which is not justified by the evidence.

What might be seen as the subjective, experiential, or social psychological aspect of class research has attracted considerable interest since the 1940s in both Britain and the United States. While the theoretical basis of class research is different in the two countries, as we noted in Chapter 1, nevertheless research into subjective aspects of class/status has taken a roughly parallel course on both sides of the Atlantic. The two basic issues seem to have been class consciousness – i.e. the identification of class and the sense of 'belonging' – and whether people see society as structured into bounded classes (i.e. middle-class, working-class) or as a continuous status hierarchy. Interest has centred on 'problems' such as 'false class consciousness' (especially in the working class) and differences in imagery between working-class and middle-class people.

Researchers have argued that it is important to study the subjective as well as the objective aspects of class – that is, to find out how people actually experience social inequalities. Here it is important to keep in mind the difference between class awareness and class consciousness: people can be aware of inequalities and even resent them without thereby necessarily acquiring a sense of belonging to a class. Alternatively, people can identify with a social class without being aware of underlying inequalities. Furthermore, it is difficult to determine precisely how respondents actually see the social world and what the class labels actually mean to them. Nevertheless it is generally accepted that individuals' self-assignment to a social class is an acceptable first approximation to describing how they locate themselves in the social structure, and that this placement has implications both for self-image and for individual beliefs and actions.

The relationship between subjective and objective aspects of class is a theoretical problematic. Theorists have been concerned with the issue at least in part because of the distinction Marx made between objective and subjective aspects of class – between a class in itself and a class for itself. While this has been an important point of reference for much research, most have been influenced by Weberian theory. Thus most research in this tradition has stressed the importance of the manual/non-manual divide – a division that is of little theoretical significance for Marxists in terms of collective class action. Weberians equate class position with market situation rather than relationship to the means of production and argue that the manual/non-manual divide is of considerable importance because it forms a strong barrier to social mobility both inter- and intragenerationally. Furthermore, the research on subjective social class indicates that in assigning themselves and other people to classes individuals take into account factors other than occupation (e.g. income level, educational qualifications, and so on). In this context Weber makes the important distinction between the class/status of individuals and the status of communal groups and stresses the importance of communal action and group identification. Finally, Marx was concerned with classes as collectivities, while the research on subjective class has, of course, been more concerned with the views of individuals, although these have often have often been related to issues about collectivities – e.g. by Lockwood (1958), Goldthorpe *et al*. (1969), Bulmer (1975). However, Wright (1985) has argued from a neo-Marxist perspective that there has been a debate within Marxism over what class consciousness is. He suggests that there are two competing positions within the Marxist tradition: those (for example, Lukács) who argue that class consciousness is an important characteristic of classes as collectivities, and the tradition Wright develops in his own work of seeing class consciousness strictly as an attribute of individuals. Thus research can be conducted into the subjectivity of individuals by examining their beliefs, ideas, theories, preferences, and so on; from within this perspective Wright is concerned to examine the class consciousness of manual workers and of different non-manual groups and to draw conclusions about their degree of class polarization.

We can see, then, that overall class theory has played an important part in influencing research into subjective social class awareness. However, there are theoretical and practical issues which are in dispute between researchers, and these will be dealt with in more detail below as they become relevant to the points under discussion. The main point that needs to be made here, before examining the findings of previous research and comparing them with an analysis of the People in Society Survey, is that most previous researchers have either interviewed only men or, where women have been included in the sample, have determined the objective class of the women not from their own occupations but from those of their 'head of household' (for the vast majority of women their husband or their father). In recent years, however, some research has tended to suggest that husband's occupation is not the best and certainly not the only indicator of women's social class. In the United States addressing this issue Jackman and Jackman (1983) have argued that a wife's socio-economic characteristics are unimportant in class identification. However, Ritter and Hargens (1975) found evidence to sustain the view that an employed wife's own occupational status is as important as her husband's in determining her class identification. Hiller and Philliber (1982) found support for this hypothesis, and the results of Van Velso and Beeghley (1979) suggest that employed married women use a combination of own, husband's, and father's characteristics in assessing their own status. (Non-employed wives, they argue, do 'borrow' their husband's status.) While denying the importance of own occupation, Jackman and Jackman found a wife's education to be a significant factor. In a previous analysis of part of the People in Society data-set (Abbott and Sapsford 1986) we found that both own occupation and educational characteristics are significant factors along with husband's occupation. We also found that where a woman's own occupation would place her in a higher class than her husband's, husband's status did not significantly influence subjective class identification. In view of this evidence it seems unsafe to ignore any longer the implications of a woman's own characteristics in determining her social class identification, class orientation, and class action. On the contrary, a married woman may influence her husband as much as he influences her, both in terms of the attitudes and values she develops from her work experience and of the consumption class enjoyed by her household (see Dale, Gilbert, and Arber 1983).

Own class and head of household's

A preliminary question is the extent to which 'social class' is a meaningful common-language term as well as a concept in the social sciences. Are social classes groups that exist in the public consciousness, terms of everyday discourse, and if they do exist in this sense then how do people identify, define, and understand them? As Jackman and Jackman (1983) have argued, these are empirical questions, not ones susceptible to a priori answers. Research in Britain and the United States since the Second World War sugests a general awareness of social class in the populace and that social class labels are used with some frequency. Indeed, use of the concept of social class is found even in research not specifically concerned with it; for example, Reid (1980), interviewing teachers on subjects other than social class, found very frequent references to social class and social imagery on his tapes. We need, then, to explore the extent to which women recognize the existence of social classes, what they see as the criteria for membership of the different classes, and what factors are related to subjective social class identification.

There is, in fact, some evidence of considerable consensus among men on who belongs in which class, in terms of the job they perform – men agree substantially on a ranking of occupations in terms of social class. Hall and Jones (1950), constructing the Hall-Jones Scale, asked respondents to order hierarchically a list of occupations; there was considerable agreement between respondents' rankings and a high correspondence between the rankings of respondents and a prior ranking by Hall and Jones. Goldthorpe and Hope (1974), in constructing the social class scale used in the Oxford Mobility Study, also asked respondents to rank occupations: they asked for forty male occupations to be ranked according to four criteria – standard of living, qualifications, power/influence over other people, and value to society. Respondents found little difficulty, it is reported, in carrying out the task, there was a high degree of agreement, and a rerun two to three months later found considerable stability of ranking. In the main study respondents were asked to rank occupational titles according to their social standing, and again there was considerable agreement. (There is also evidence from research in the United States that men and women tend to agree in their rankings – see Bose 1973; Treiman 1977.) However, it should be noted that despite high overall agreement most studies uncover some respondents very much at variance with the majority. This was certainly the case in the Goldthorpe and Hope work, and Young and Willmott (1956) found some manual workers who considered that manual workers ought to be ranked alongside doctors and above lawyers and managers. Also, Coxon and Jones (1978) have questioned what agreement on occupational ranking among respondents actually means. They suggest that it does *not* necessarily mean that people share the same perception or cognition of the occupations ranked.

Nevertheless it does suggest that there is some agreement on the relative social status of occupations – although it must be noted that in general researchers have asked respondents to rank *male* occupations. Where both sexes were included as objects of ranking in research in the United States, Haavio-Manilla (1969) found that respondents consistently scored males higher than females in the same occupation, and the wives of men in the occupation lower than employed females. However, she eliminated the possibility of equal scoring by requiring respondents not to produce tied ranks. Bose (1973) found that men and women in the same occupation were accorded the same level of prestige, and England (1979) in addition found no evidence to sustain the view that occupations scored lower when they were female-dominated; they had a prestige score predictable from their level of complexity and training requirements.

Finally, to show that people can place occupations in a consistent order of prestige does not demonstrate an awareness of classes as bounded collectivities. Nor does it tell us what is used as the basis of the ranking, nor on what basis respondents allocate other individuals to class/status positions – whether they use occupation alone or whether other factors are also seen as relevant.

Researchers have also found agreement among the general public on the *fact* that there are classes in society, and even a strong tendency to nominate 'classes' spontaneously as groups that exist in society. In the People in Society Survey 35 per cent of the female respondents spontaneously mentioned social class when asked about groups in society to which they belonged, and 92.5 per cent agreed that classes exist when asked the question direct. These are much the same figures as have been reported in previous research on both male and female samples (Martin 1954; NOP 1972; Reid 1977; Townsend 1979; and in the United States Jackman and Jackman 1983). Previous researchers have also found that a high percentage of the population are prepared to place themselves in a social class and that the vast majority use the terms 'middle' or 'working' when doing so (Martin 1954; Runciman 1964; Kahan *et al.* 1966). Townsend in

Britain (1979) and Jackman and Jackman in the United States (1983), however, found that men were more likely to refer to themselves as working-class and women more likely to place themselves in the middle class. The data for the female respondents in the People in Society Survey give similar results: 50 per cent place themselves in the middle class, about 32 per cent in the working class, with 18 per cent giving a different response (about 12 per cent qualifying the term 'middle', five per cent qualifying 'working', and relatively tiny proportions describing themselves as 'upper' or 'lower'). Previous research has also found that when given a prompted or forced choice the majority of respondents can and do place themselves in one of the two categories 'middle class' or 'working class', and the same was true in the People in Society Survey: only 52 women refused to answer, about 58 per cent called themselves middle-class, and about 42 per cent working-class.

The distinction also appears to have meaning in the sense that respondents do think there is a difference between the middle class and the working class. An innovative feature of Jane Henry's design of the survey was the inclusion of semantic differential scales (see Chapter 2). An analysis of the responses on this data set suggests that respondents do see the two classes as having different characteristics and different positions in life. Over 90 per cent of the female respondents indicated differences between the middle and the working class in the expected direction (though median size of difference was not large).

However, these results only suggest that people are prepared to place themselves in social classes which they see as differing from one another – not on what basis they do so. Researchers usually assign social class to individuals on the basis of their occupation, although married women are generally assigned on the basis of their husbands' occupations, and it is generally found that a majority of respondents place themselves 'correct-ly' – that is, in the category in which the researcher places them. Strongest agreement is found at the extremes and least in the middle of the hierarchy. Thus a substantial number of respon-dents, though an overall minority, appear to misclassify them-selves, especially in the intermediate classes (see Martin 1954; Runciman 1964; Butler and Stokes 1974; Roberts *et al*. 1977; Townsend 1979; and for the United States Jackman and

Jackman 1983). While there appears to be a definite break at the manual/non-manual divide, in some research only a bare majority of routine non-manual workers have placed themselves in the middle class (e.g. Butler and Stokes 1974; Roberts *et al.* 1977; Townsend 1979), and in the United States Jackman and Jackman found that only 40 per cent of clerical workers saw themselves as middle-class. Furthermore, some researchers find that women up-rate their social class over the researcher's categorization more than men do (e.g. Martin 1954), but this finding is not always replicated (see e.g. Runciman 1964). Townsend (1979) found that husbands and wives generally placed themselves in the same social class and that the majority of discrepancies could be accounted for by taking into account the current or previous occupation of the wife. Thus it could be argued that any apparent tendency among women to over-rate their class position may be because at least some women married to manual workers identify their class position in terms of their own current or previous middle-class job. It also seems highly likely that the gender difference in the overall proportion claiming to be middle-class is accounted for by the difference between genders in the distribution of available jobs by class.

Of the *men* in the People in Society Survey, 55.5 per cent defined themselves as middle-class and 44.5 as working-class. On the basis of 'objective class' – the Social Grading Scheme – about 28 per cent uprated their class and about 21 per cent downrated it (see *Table 28*). In general those at the extremes are less likely to 'misplace' themselves than those in intermediate groups. Nevertheless the manual/routine non-manual divide seems to form a definite 'cross-over point' in the figures; while about two-thirds of those in routine non-manual jobs say they see themselves as middle-class, less than a third of those in skilled manual jobs do so. Looking at the female respondents, we find comparable results. If we compare subjective social class with head of household's class, we find that about 60 per cent of the women define themselves as middle-class and around 40 per cent as working-class. On this basis 31 per cent 'uprate' themselves and 19 per cent 'downrate' themselves (see *Table 29*). Furthermore, there is little difference if we use own rather than head of household's job as a basis of comparison (*Table 30*) for those women currently in employment.

Table 28 Self-assigned and own class of men in the survey (%)

subjective class	own occupational class					summary	
	A	*B*	*C1*	*C2*	*D*	*ABC1*	*C2D*
Middle	95.4	80.2	66.3	30.6	24.8	79.1	28.3
Working	4.6	19.8	33.7	69.4	75.2	20.9	71.7

Table 29 Assignment of female respondents to middle or working class: self, and head of household's occupation (%)

self-assignment	head of household's occupation	
	middle	working
Middle	80.6	31.2
Working	19.4	68.8
As percentage of all female respondents		
Middle	45.9	13.4
Working	11.0	29.6

Table 30 Assignment of employed female respondents to middle or working class: self, and own occupation (%)

self-assignment	own occupation	
	middle	working
Middle	77.7	30.5
Working	22.3	69.5
As percentage of all employed female respondents		
Middle	49.0	11.3
Working	14.0	25.7

Most of the recent controversy over class placement has concerned the class to be ascribed to married women, but it is also important to consider those who are not married. *Single* women have conventionally been placed in an 'objective' class according to the class of a 'head of household' who might be themselves, their fathers, a man they happened to be living with, or another male or sometimes female relative. In the People in Society five-year data set there were 612 respondents who were female, single, and in paid employment, of whom 262 were classified as head of household. Sixty-six per cent of these single women saw themselves as middle-class and 34 per cent as working-class. Head of household's class correlates significantly (dichotomized at the manual/non-manual divide) with subjective class placement, but own occupational class shows a much stronger correlation (see *Table 31*). Multiple regression analysis suggests that head of household's class has nothing of significance to add to the prediction of subjective class once own occupation has been taken into account. (As the two 'objective' measures are identical for women who are themselves head of household, the difference is, of course, stronger for women who are not.) Thus for single women in employment it seems that own occupation is a better basis for classification than the occupation of the head of household. The overall distribution of single working women with respect to the two objective measures is shown in *Tables 32* and *33*.

The situation for married women is more complex. As we saw in Chapter 1, much of the current debate surrounding women and social class has been concerned precisely with how we determine the social class position of married women. The conventional position is that a married woman, whether or not in paid employment, should be classified according to the class of her husband. In contradistinction to this it has been argued that either a composite index of social class should be constructed, based on the occupations of both husband and wife, or alternatively that a married woman's own characteristics should be used in determining her class position. In our data (for married women currently living with their partners – we shall consider separately the divorced, widowed, and separated) we have occupational information only for men and for women currently in employment, so we shall look at employed and non-employed women separately in considering these possibilities. This would in any case be necessary even if we knew the previous occupation of currently non-employed women, because an actual current occupation may have a different impact on class placement from that of a job left some time in the past – especially if the woman has been economically inactive for a considerable time. (Note, however, that Dale *et al.* (1983) have argued that occupation prior to first withdrawal from the labour market is a reasonable measure of social class for women – see Chapter 1.)

Table 31 Single employed women: Correlation of 'objective' measures with self-assigned class according to whether or not head of household

correlation with	total	head of household	not head of household
Own occupation	0.58	0.48	0.63
Head of household's occupation	0.39	0.48	0.23
Numbers in sample	612	262	350

Table 32 Employed single women: Own occupation and self-assigned class (%)

self-assigned class	own occupational class					
	A	B	C1	C2	D	total
Middle	92.9	86.1	79.9	30.4	32.1	65.9
Working	7.1	13.9	20.1	69.6	67.9	34.1

Table 33 Employed single women: Head of household's occupation and self-assigned class (%)

self-assigned class	head of household's occupation					
	A	B	C1	C2	D	total
Middle	91.7	86.8	83.7	47.4	20.0	75.1
Working	8.3	13.2	16.3	52.6	80.0	24.9

There were 1,130 married working women in the five-year People in Society data set. Of these, 57 per cent called themselves middle-class and 43 per cent working-class. Husband's occupation and own occupation are both strongly related to the class in which the women place themselves (see *Tables 34* and *35*). Women with husbands in middle-class occupations are much more likely to see themselves as middle-class than women with working-class husbands, and the converse, of course, holds for the latter; the same pattern appears when we look at the distribution by own occupation. (Again it is worth noting that the pattern is stronger at the extremes than in the middle, with a clear divide or 'cross-over point' at the manual/non-manual divide.) Multivariate analysis suggests that both own

Table 34   Employed married women: Own occupation and
self-assigned class (%)

self-assigned class	own occupation					
	A	B	C1	C2	D	total
Middle	100.0	89.8	67.8	44.2	24.0	57.4
Working	—	10.2	32.4	55.8	76.0	42.6

Table 35   Employed married women: Head of household's
occupation and self-assigned class (%)

self-assigned class	head of household's occupation					
	A	B	C1	C2	D	total
Middle	89.5	84.9	64.3	31.0	18.8	57.4
Working	10.5	15.1	35.7	69.0	81.3	42.6

and husband's class can contribute independently to the
prediction of subjective class placement – husband's class rather
more strongly than own class, but the difference is not large.
The situation is broadly the same whether the women are
working full-time or part-time, though the difference in predictive value is very slightly larger in the latter case; whether the
current job is a full-time or a part-time one does not seem to be
an important influence on the power of own occupation to
predict subjective class placement.

Table 36 looks at the relative importance of husband's and own
occupational class as predictors of subjective class placement for
married working women, using correlations based on dichotomized class scales (middle *vs* working class). As will be seen,
husband's class is the best overall predictor, but own occupation
adds significantly to the prediction: the multiple correlation is
significantly higher than either of the zero-order ones. Moreover, multicollinearity clouds the analysis in that the zero-order
correlations of own and husband's occupation with the criterion
variable are both substantial and not very different in size, and
the two are more highly intercorrelated than the correlation of
either with the criterion. We shall see, later in the chapter, that
a different and more complex picture emerges when other
variables are entered into the analysis and when such analysis is

Table 36 All employed women: Intercorrelation of own and head of household's class with self-assigned class

class	self-assigned	class head of household	own occupation
Self-assigned	1	0.54	0.47
Head of household		1	0.65
Own occupation			1

Note
Multiple correlation with self-assigned class: $r = 0.558$.

carried out separately for cross-class marriages (as it is essentially meaningless in same-class marriages, where by definition the class of husband and wife are the same). On the basis of this and the last two tables it would appear that for working married women their own occupation is more or less as good an indicator of what broad social class they see themselves in as their husband's occupation (which was also the conclusion of the Ritter and Hargens paper).

Doubts have been raised as to whether this kind of comparison – split conventionally into a 'middle class' and a 'working class' at the manual/non-manual divide – is as meaningful for women as for men, as we saw in Chapter 2: the hierarchical ordering of the component classes is by no means as obviously justified, and there is indeed some evidence (e.g. Webb 1985) that women may rate skilled manual work above some work conventionally classified as routine non-manual. Following Ritter's and Hargens' analysis of American data (1975) we checked this in an earlier paper (Abbott and Sapsford 1986) by decomposing the scales into a series of discrete 'dummy variables' (dichotomies) to see if these would provide a better aggregate predictor of subjective class placement than the single hierarchical scales; the thinking behind this was that if the relationship is in fact non-linear, then each sub-class is free to contribute positively or negatively to the prediction. We found, as Ritter and Hargens did on their earlier American sample, that the more complex procedure did not improve the prediction; on the whole the scales seem to behave as if correctly ordered. (However, this does not, of course, answer the question of whether *particular* jobs are misclassified within the scales.)

Noting that a very large proportion of the married working women in the sample had jobs in the same category as their husbands (*Table 37*), thereby confounding own class with husband's, we looked to see what happened in the cross-class marriages. Overall we found 42.4 per cent of these women in the same occupational class as their husband's job would suggest, 44.6 per cent in a lower class than their husbands, and 13 per cent in a higher one. *Table 38* shows the results of multiple regression separately for these three groups. For those with husbands in a higher occupation than their own, husband's occupation and own occupation both showed substantial correlations with subjective class – husband's occupation having the higher correlation, though the difference is not large – and both make an independent contribution to the prediction of subjective class. For those in the same class as their husbands, both variables again predict subjective class, but they are by definition equal, so one cannot speak of one making a contribution distinct from the other's. The surprising finding came when we looked at women with husbands in a lower occupation than

Table 37 Employed married women: Occupational class of husband and wife

class of husband		*A*	*B*	class of wife *C1*	*C2*	*D*	Summary: husband's class	
A	%	1.4	3.2	5.1	0.7	0.6	Lower	13.0
B	%	0.1	14.7	14.6	1.8	1.2	Same	42.4
C1	%	—	1.7	8.6	1.8	1.2	Higher	44.6
C2	%	—	0.8	8.1	7.8	14.3		
D	%	—	0.1	1.6	0.5	10.0		

Table 38 Employed married women in cross-class marriages: Correlation of objective class indicators with self-assigned class

class indicator	*own class*	*husband's*	*both*
Husband's class higher	0.51	0.53	0.59
Husband's class lower	−0.02	0.28	0.28

their own: here husband's class is a poor predictor (accounting for only about 8 per cent of the variance), but the correlation of own occupation with subjective class does not even reach statistical significance. The interim conclusion, therefore, in contradiction to what was suggested above, is that husband's class is on the whole a better predictor of a married working woman's subjective class than her own current job. (This conclusion will be modified below, however, where other variables are taken into the equation.)

When we look at full-time housewives we again find a strong relationship between subjective social class and husband's occupation (*Table 39*), again stronger at the extremes and with a clear cross-over point at the manual/non-manual divide. Dichotomized husband's class correlates strongly with subjective class placement – r = 0.51, accounting for 25.4 per cent of the variance. Surprisingly, however, this is lower than the value obtained for *working* married women, where 28.8 per cent of the variance was accounted for by husband's occupational class.

The final group to consider are the divorced, widowed, and separated, who are generally counted as head of their own household and therefore conventionally classified according to their own occupations. Here we again find a strong relationship between subjective and objective social class, though this is not as strong as found in the other groups of women, particularly for those in semi- and unskilled employment, as can be seen from *Table 40*. The correlation between dichotomized occupational class and subjective class is statistically significant at the 0.01 level, but low in comparison to other groups – r = 0.25. It is not immediately apparent why this should be the case. Possibly these women are forced by their circumstances to take work below the level that they might otherwise have achieved, or

Table 39 Full-time housewives: Husband's occupational class and self-assigned class (%)

self-assigned class	class of husband					
	A	B	C1	C2	D	total
Middle	93.9	88.2	51.2	38.6	15.1	58.2
Lower	6.1	11.8	48.8	61.4	84.9	41.8

Table 40   Divorced, widowed, or separated women:
Occupational class and self-assigned class (%)

self-assigned class	occupational class					
	A	B	C1	C2	D	total
Middle	100.0	75.8	59.7	33.3	19.2	44.4
Working	—	24.2	40.3	66.7	67.7	55.6

perhaps below the level of a significant other from whom they
'borrow' their subjective class placement – father, perhaps, or
even ex-husband. Indeed, this raises a point of general relevance to the other groups we have examined, for although the
relationship is stronger there, most of the variance in subjective
class placement is still *not* accounted for. This could be explained
in part by a tendency for married women to take (or to be forced
to take) jobs below what they would consider their true level
(see Chapters 1 and 3). This 'true level' and what contributes to
it can be explored best by looking at other factors which contribute to subjective class placement, and this is attempted in the
next section.

Other factors

Previous research has provided strong evidence that factors
other than marital, occupational, and/or original class are
important in the determination of subjective class placement.
Runciman (1964) found that income, father's occupation, and
geographical region were all relevant factors. In the United
States Jackman and Jackman (1983) found that for both men and
women the occupation of the head of household was the most
important factor, but that education and household income also
contributed; these three variables together explained 27 per cent
of the variance in subjective social class identification. For
married women they found that a woman's own occupation had
little or no effect on her or her husband's social class identification – that she 'borrowed' her status from her husband to a
considerable extent. However, they did find that women's own
educational level made a significant contribution to their class
identification. This is an important point, as a wife receives her

education mostly *before* she marries her husband, so to assert that married women's status is entirely borrowed from their husbands is to ignore, in the face of the evidence, the importance of their own background. Furthermore, Jackman and Jackman found that background as assessed from father's occupational class also made a significant contribution; when father's class was added to the multiple regression predicting subjective class the variance explained rose from 27 per cent to 34 per cent , a quite substantial increase.

The People in Society Survey, in addition to own and head of household's occupation, included questions on father's occupation, own and head of household's income, age at leaving school (from which we have computed 'years of post-compulsory schooling'), and educational qualifications. We were able, therefore, to include all these variables in multiple regression analyses to try to determine the relative importance of each factor in determining subjective class identification and to find the total amount of variance that the factors taken together could explain. It is important to note multicollinearity, however – the factors are often highly intercorrelated and thus may function as alternative indicators. We have already noted the high correlation of own with husband's occupational class for economically active married women, and that one or the other – not always readily separated, because of the intercorrelation – acts as an important predictor of subjective class. The causal links are not beyond doubt, however; it may be that some people choose their occupation on the basis of how they see themselves. Similarly, one is inclined to argue that educational variables are in a sense 'causal', but decisions about staying on at school and taking educational qualifications could again be influenced in some people by an already well-formed self-image. Indeed, choice of husband (or availability of certain types of men in the 'pool' of potential husbands) may itself be determined by prior self-image or by educational or occupational decisions. We shall return to these points later.

As when analysing the relationship of occupational class to subjective class, we shall look at groups of women separately. We have already seen that *single* women's occupational class is an important factor in determining the class in which they place themselves. However, multiple regression demonstrates that other factors are also influential: class of father, qualifications, and years of post-compulsory schooling all make a significant contribution. In fact these factors plus occupation explain 40 per cent of the variance; occupation alone explains only 33 per cent (see *Table 41*). (There is a high degree of intercorrelation between the four factors, however.) If we look separately at single women who are classified as heads of household we find a slightly different picture. Occupation is the most important predictor, accounting for 23 per cent of the variance, but only two of the other variables make a significant additional contribution – class of father and years of post-compulsory education. The picture changes yet again when we look at single women who are *not* heads of household: the total amount of variance explained is considerably higher (51 per cent), and own class, father's class and educational qualifications are the contributing variables. The two subgroups are compared in *Table 42*.

When we looked at *married* women we found that husband's occupation was a better predictor of subjective social class than own occupation for employed women, irrespective of whether they were employed full- or part-time; this also held true for women in cross-class marriages. Taking other factors into account, however, we find that the combination which explains the most variance (over 35 per cent) contains, in order of entry: class of husband, years of post-compulsory education, husband's income (making a contribution independent of husband's class), own class, class of father, and educational qualifications (making a small contribution independent of the other educational variable). If we omit husband's class we can still explain 34 per cent of the variance, but if we use only the three 'class' variables we can explain only 32 per cent. If we force

Table 41   Single women: Prediction of self-assigned class

stepwise multiple regression: variables entered	multiple correlation	% variance explained	beta coefficient in final equation
Class of own job	0.58	33.5	0.371
Class of father	0.61	36.6	0.187
Educational qualifications	0.63	39.5	0.158
Post-compulsory education	0.64	40.0	0.045

Table 42 Single women: Prediction of self-assigned class by whether or not head of household

zero-order correlations with self-assigned class	head of household	not head of household
variables		
Own class	0.48	0.63
Post-compulsory schooling	0.45	0.46
Educational qualifications	0.39	0.41
Class of father	0.36	0.39
Income	0.33	0.45
Class of head of household		0.23

Multiple correlation	Correlation	% variance explained	Correlation	% variance explained
variables				
Own class	0.48	23.1	0.63	39.9
Post-compulsory schooling	0.52	26.8		
Educational qualifications			0.68	45.9
Class of father	0.54	27.8	0.72	50.9

wife's occupation into the equation as prime variable and then remove it on the last step the variance explained drops by 0.7 per cent – a small amount but statistically significant, confirming that wife's class does make an independent contribution over and above the effects of all the other variables.

A similar picture emerges if we confine the analysis to women in *full*-time employment. Again husband's employment is the main factor, accounting for 26 per cent of the variance; wife's occupation on its own accounts for only 21 per cent. However, husband's occupation is not as important as for the group of married women as a whole when other variables are entered into the equation – post-compulsory schooling, own class, class of father, husband's income, and own educational qualifications (to list them in order of contribution) – and own class assumes a rather greater importance. These factors together explain about

Table 43 Employed married women: Prediction of self-assigned class

zero-order correlation with self-assigned class	correlation	% variance explained
Class of husband	0.54	29.6
Husband's income	0.41	16.6
Own class	0.47	22.9
Educational qualifications	0.44	19.4
Class of father	0.36	13.0
Post-compulsory education	0.47	21.8
Own income	0.23	5.2
multiple correlation	0.60	35.8
Beta coefficients in final equation		
Husband's class	0.224	
Husband's income	0.154	
Own class	0.123	
Educational qualifications	0.111	
Post-compulsory education	0.094	
Father's class	0.093	
multiple correlation excluding own class	0.59	34.9
Beta coefficients in final equation		
Husband's class	0.274	
Husband's income	0.161	
Educational qualifications	0.128	
Post-compulsory education	0.108	
Father's class	0.102	

36 per cent of the variance. With women in *part*-time employment we can explain about 31 per cent of the variance, with husband's occupation as the most important variable, followed by own class, husband's income, father's class, and the two educational variables.

Thus we can see that for married women both their own and their husband's characteristics help to account for their subjective class identification, but that husband's occupation comes out consistently as the major determinant. The variables are strongly intercorrelated, however, and, as we noted above, a large proportion of the women are in the same occupational class as their husbands, thereby confounding the two variables. We can look, however, at the extent to which husband's class is dominant specifically in cross-class marriages, and the results of doing so are shown in *Table 44*. For those whose husband's occupation was 'higher' than their own, the largest predictor was husband's class, followed by husband's income, class of father, own class, and post-compulsory education. (Note, however, that the zero-order correlations of own and husband's class with subjective class are virtually identical.) For women who are in the same occupational class as their husbands, the husband's occupational class enters the equation first, followed by his income and her years of post-compulsory education; note, however, both that husband's and own class are by definition

Table 44 Employed married women: Prediction of self-assigned class in cross-class marriages

zero-order correlation with self-assigned class	*own class in relation to husband's*					
	same		*higher*		*lower*	
	r	*% variance*	*r*	*% variance*	*r*	*% variance*
Class of husband	0.60	36	0.53	28	0.28	8
Class of father	0.32	10	0.45	20	0.18	3
Own class	0.60	36	0.51	26	0.02	—
Educational qualifications	0.52	27	0.35	12	0.42	18
Post-compulsory education	0.52	27	0.47	22	0.23	5
Own income	0.26	7	0.21	4	0.16	3
Husband's income	0.41	18	0.49	24	0.01	—
multiple correlation						
Multiple r	0.62	39	0.64	41	0.42	18

variables entered:			
	Own class (= husband's) Husband's income Post-compulsory education	Husband's class Husband's income Father's class Own class Post-compulsory education	Educational qualifications

identical, and that the zero-order correlations of the educational variables with subjective class are actually significantly higher than the correlation of husband's income. Finally, where the husband is in a 'lower' class than the wife the pattern changes completely. The only variable to make a significant entry into the analysis is educational qualifications, which explains about 18 per cent of the variance, and husband's class does not add anything significant to this. It is clear, then, that the overall trends conceal considerable variation.

We can also ask, in cross-class marriages, if husband's occupation explains 'deviant' subjective class identification as measured against own job for married working women. We did indeed find that when women thought of themselves as middle-class when own job would place them in the working class, class of husband was the only statistically significant explanation, but that it did not constitute a substantively satisfactory explanation; the zero-order correlation was low ($r = 0.17$), explaining a negligible proportion of the variance (not much more than 3 per cent). When we looked at women who would be middle-class by their own job but saw themselves as working-class, we again found a correlation with husband's job, but a much higher one ($r = 0.51$), and father's class also showed a significant zero-order correlation ($r = 0.31$). The two together explained about 30 per cent of the variance.

We have seen that when looking at working married women, class of husband is consistently a better predictor of self-assigned class than own occupation (except in the case of women whose own occupational class is higher than that of their husbands, where educational variables appear to be the only indicator). However, the difference in zero-order correlation is never large, and own occupational class generally makes a significant independent contribution to the prediction. We can conclude that husband's and own occupation contribute independently to the explanation of subjective class assignment, as indeed does class of father. When educational variables relating to the wife – years of post-compulsory education and qualifications achieved – are included in the analysis, a substantially more accurate prediction is achieved. In particular, years of post-compulsory schooling tends to rival husband's class in the size of its effect, and it pushes wife's occupation well down the list of predictive variables. This result confirms the findings of others (e.g. Heath and Britten 1984), suggests that education is an important source of class sentiment, and points the way towards a possible means of assigning an 'occupational' class to women who do not currently have paid employment (i.e. housewives).

When we broke down the sample by the relationship of husband's occupational class to wife's a different and more complex picture emerged. For women in the same class as their husbands, their joint class was the best predictor of self-assigned class, with husband's income and years of post-compulsory education adding something independently to the prediction. For women whose current occupation was lower than that of their husband, husband's class was the best predictor, followed by husband's income, class of father, own class, and years of post-compulsory schooling. For those whose current occupation was higher than that of their husband, only educational qualifications made a difference; class of husband made no contribution to the prediction. The conclusion would appear to be that overall education is as important a predictor as class of own occupation, and that different factors come into play depending on the relationship of own job to husband's.

Taking these results into account, however, and also the high degree of intercorrelation between husband's occupation, own occupation, years of post-compulsory education, and qualifications obtained, it seems to us that a more radical position might be adopted. It is commonplace in empirical analyses of propensity to crime that all the plausible 'causes of crime' which one may put into a predictive analysis of re-offending are swamped by 'number of previous convictions', as though having been caught three times rather than four or five was the only variable showing a large and genuine causal relationship with the likelihood of re-offending or being caught again. Few criminologists really believe this conclusion, however. What seems more likely is that, over and above any genuine causal influence, 'previous convictions' acts as a 'summary' for all the other factors of background and history which might be related to re-offending; they are all so highly related to previous convictions, and to each other, that when previous convictions enters the equation it effectively accounts for these other

variables as well. Similarly, where years of schooling or qualifications obtained displace wife's occupational class in the prediction of self-assigned class, at least part of the reason is likely
to be that wife's occupation is highly correlated with the education variables. An interaction effect also appears: what relates to
women's self-assigned class changes according to the relationship of their own occupations to those of their husbands.

One might go further and point to the high level of correlation
of *husband's* class with wife's class – the two are identical for over
40 per cent of the sample – and with the education variables.
One should remember, furthermore, that lives are not lived at
random: people who stay on at school longer and/or obtain
qualifications tend towards certain kinds of jobs. This in turn
alters the nature of the 'pool' of people they are likely to meet
and become friendly with, and thus in turn affects the class of
the person they are likely to marry. There is a substantial
literature on the affects of propinquity/availability on friendship
and marriage (e.g. Abrams 1943; Athanasiou and Yoshika 1973;
Bossard 1932; Ebbesen, Kjos and Konecni 1976; Katz and Hill
1958; Seagoe 1933); most of this is concerned with area of
residence, but type of employment must surely have a similar
influence. Prandy's recent work (1986) certainly appears to
demonstrate very distinct patterning in mate selection, particularly if conventional categories are decomposed into more
meaningful units in terms of actual job performed and therefore
who is met, rather than overall notions of skill and market
position; mate selection is clearly far from random, but on the
contrary there are 'typical' marriage patterns for those who hold
particular kinds of jobs – differing from job to job in sometimes
illuminating ways.

One might indeed go further still and suggest that level of
education and type of job obtained both reflect, in middle-class
women at least, a prior commitment to a certain set of attitudes
and values, and/or constitute stages of a 'filtering process'
which selectively narrows the range of men from among whom
they are likely to find a husband. If this argument is accepted,
however, it must be taken as implying that analyses such as
the current one, looking cross-sectionally at possible determinants of occupation or self-assigned class, can *never* answer
the questions they set out to ask, because they can never demon-

strate determinants – only correlates, with no clear idea of the direction (if any) of causation. If it be accepted that the likelihood of a woman's marrying one kind of man rather than another is influenced by the education she has received and the job she holds, one is debarred from then using husband's occupational class as an independent variable in analysis of wife's class position; the two are related not causally, but as aspects of the same single phenomenon.

To summarize, we have argued that for single women, whether or not they are classified as head of household, their own characteristics are the best predictor of subjective social class identification, and that for working married women they are also an important factor to be taken into account – and, indeed, that it makes little sense to ask whether own or husband's characteristics are more important in a causal sense, given the interrelationship of competing predictors and the way they can be seen as forming essentially inseparable parts of a single life-course. This still leaves full-time housewives to be considered. We have already seen that husband's occupation explains some 25 per cent of the variance in subjective class assignment among this group, and that this (paradoxically) is less than the amount explained among employed married women. We can increase the proportion of variance explained to nearly 36 per cent – roughly the same percentage as was explained for working married women – by multivariate regression, including (in order of importance) husband's class, years of post-compulsory schooling, husband's income, and class of father. If husband's class is removed from the equation we continue to explain over 32 per cent of the variance; all three of the other variables increase their contribution and remain in the same order of importance. If we go on to remove husband's income from the equation as well the percentage drops to not much more than 27 per cent. Note, however, that this 27 per cent of variance is what is explained by wife's characteristics alone, and that it is more than is explained by husband's class alone (see *Table 45*).

Finally, the women recorded as 'divorced, widowed, or separated' presented a puzzle. We have already indicated that own occupation correlated significantly with subjective social class and explained a statistically significant amount of the

Table 45 Full-time housewives: Prediction of self-assigned class

zero-order correlations with self-assigned class	correlation	% variance explained
Class of husband	0.51	25.4
Post-compulsory education	0.49	23.8
Educational qualifications	0.35	12.1
Husband's income	0.41	16.9
Class of father	0.41	16.4
multiple correlation		
variables entered:		
Class of husband	0.51	25.4
Post-compulsory education	0.56	31.3
Husband's income	0.58	33.3
Class of father	0.60	35.9

variance – but so small an amount in absolute terms as to be substantively uninteresting. Entering the other variables in a multiple regression analysis, we found that none correlated significantly with subjective social class and none explained any portion of the variance once the effects of own occupation had been taken into account. All we can conclude is that the size of the sample is too small to show complex relationships, or that the wrong variables have been collected in this case, or most likely that the group is so heterogeneous that it is a mistake to look for common explanations within it.

Our analysis of women's self-assignment to middle or working class has indicated that a woman's own characteristics are important in determining how she places herself. While for those women who are married and living with their husbands his occupation and income are relevant factors, they are not the only relevant factors even for this group, and this holds true whether or not the woman is currently in employment of her own. Given that background characteristics are acquired before women acquire their husbands, we feel that a wife's own characteristics must be taken into account in determining her class position. This does not, of course, mean that a partner's characteristics are of no relevance, but that it is unsound to treat them as the only relevant factors. It seems clear, moreover, that a woman's class identification is influenced by her market class as well as her consumption class (see Chapter 1).

We have also established that women do make a distinction between the working class and the middle class – that they do see a difference between the two broad classes both in terms of characteristics and of lifestyle. However, we have not yet considered how the women *understand* social stratification – that is, what their image of society is and how this relates both to their own subjective social class and to their 'objective' position in the hierarchy. This will be the focus of the next two chapters.

5 The perception of class

The results discussed in the last chapter echo those of previous research: the women respondents in the People in Society Survey do see society as divided into classes, they are prepared to place themselves in a social class, and the majority (even without prompting) describe themselves as either middle- or working-class. Examining how they typified the two classes on semantic differential scales, we found that they do see a difference between the two classes – very much in the expected direction, though often not large – and that they tend to place themselves nearer in terms of descriptive attributes to the class to which they assign themselves than to the other class. None of this tells us, however, how these women see the social structure, or how they determine what class they are in and place others in the stratification hierarchy. It seems entirely likely that there will be a fairly sharp distinction between a sociological apprehension of the concept of class and the way that the concept is actually used in everyday discourse. For this reason it is important to examine social actors' consciousness of inequalities – that is, their everyday understanding of social stratification – and the relationship this bears to their social actions. Thus in this chapter and the next we examine how the women in the sample make sense of social inequalities by looking at what they see as the major determinants of class, their social imagery, and their voting behaviour, comparing our results with those of previous research. The current chapter is concerned with the perceived determinants of class and aspects of perceived social structure such as the number of classes, the possibility of social mobility, and the existence of social conflict, and with voting behaviour. The next chapter attempts to build on this analysis in more global terms, looking at the typifications or social images the women hold overall.

Dimensions and group boundaries

Two preliminary questions have to be considered before we examine how the women in the survey allocate individuals to classes. First, we need to consider whether people's everyday understanding of class in fact includes more than one dimension of stratification, and whether the questions generally used in surveys tend to force respondents to conflate these in potentially invalid or unreliable ways. Second, we need to ask whether individuals see classes as bounded groups, or whether they consider class as a continuous status hierarchy.

The first question has been largely answered by the very critics who propose it. Kluegel *et al*. (1977) attack the validity and reliability of the survey questions generally used as indicators of subjective social class, pointing out that while objective class is often conceived as multidimensional the usual questions treat subjective class very much as unidimensional. They suggest that stronger relationships than previous research has demonstrated could be obtained if subjective class were seen as a multidimensional compound, following Weber, of economic standing, lifestyle, and influence. However, they were unable to demonstrate that a multidimensional measure of social class did provide a more reliable, valid, or sensitive indicator, and they conclude in the end that subjective class is a unidimensional entity after all.

The question of whether class is to be seen as a continuous variable or in terms of bounded groups is more contentious and has been one of the major points of difference between American and European class analysis. Also of interest has been the question of the manual/non-manual divide and the extent to which routine non-manual workers are to be seen as an integral part of the middle class. Lockwood (1958) argued that male clerks were *not* falsely class-conscious when they regarded themselves as middle-class. More recent research (e.g. Davis 1979; Roberts *et al*. 1977) suggests that the majority of routine non-manual workers continue to see themselves as middle-class. However, Braverman (1980) has argued that in objective terms routine non-manual work has been undergoing a process of proletarianization for both men and women. Crompton and Jones (1984), in a study of male and female office workers, argue that because of differential chances of promotion within the office female employees are correctly seen as proletarianized but male ones are not. They suggest that this situation may change as women are no longer prepared to be 'stuck in the dead-end jobs' and come to conceive of themselves as 'having a career'.

In the People in Society Survey a majority of the women in routine non-manual employment regarded themselves as in the middle class, although the proportion was smaller than for those in professional or managerial employment (see *Tables 30* and *32* in the previous chapter). The same holds for married women whose *husbands* are in routine non-manual occupations (*Table 35*). However, the 'routine non-manual' category is made up of a number of very different occupations. Heath and Britten (1984) have suggested that female office workers are correctly identified as middle-class but that shop workers, for example, should be considered as working-class. The data on conditions of work from the OPCS survey of women in employment (Martin and Roberts 1984) lends support to this view. One of us (Abbott 1987) in a previous analysis of C1 married women in the People in Society Survey, found that husband's occupation was not the main determinant of subjective class placement and class imagery. Indeed, the results proved remarkably similar to what previous research has had to say about male routine non-manual workers. While we have already found that the majority of the women in the People in Society Survey made a distinction between the middle class and the working class, we have not yet seen where they draw that boundary – or indeed, how important it is in their view of class. Indeed, as we shall see, the evidence from the survey is ambiguous.

Previous research has suggested that the middle class tend to have a 'status' view of class, but that the working class make a clear distinction between a middle and a working class (Dahrendorf 1959; Ossowski 1963; Goldthorpe *et al.* 1969; Vanneman and Pampel 1977). Analysing American data and specifically testing whether class was seen as a continuous prestige scale or in terms of bounded groups, Vanneman and Pampel argued that the manual/non-manual divide was of considerable importance for manual workers, but less so for white-collar ones. (However, they also suggest that occupational prestige was more important for women overall.) Jackman and Jackman (1983), however, argue that their own research in the United States indicates that this divide is not of crucial importance for either manual or non-manual workers. In fact, they found that a majority of manual workers 'uprated' their own class, and that the divide did not seem to be of any great importance when respondents were given the job of sorting twelve occupations into classes. They argue, therefore, that class is seen as a continuous dimension of prestige, rather than there being 'classes' perceived as separated by the manual/non-manual divide. Similarly, Graetz (1983), analysing class images in Australia, argued that the vast majority of respondents used status criteria in assigning individuals to social classes – for example, educational qualifications, income, style of life, etc. – and he concludes, 'Generally, these distinguishing criteria are employed in a manner that enables all people to be ranked along a single social scale' (p. 87).

In the People in Society Survey we find that if we dichotomize occupational class at the manual/non-manual divide, the vast majority of the female respondents place themselves 'correctly'. About 80 per cent of those who would be classed objectively as middle-class on the basis of head of household's occupation identify themselves as middle-class, and over two-thirds of the objectively working-class women identify themselves as working-class (see *Table 29*, in the previous chapter). The results are comparable if we classify the women in employment by their own job: nearly 80 per cent of women whose jobs place them in the middle class also assign themselves to the middle class, and nearly 70 per cent of the women in manual jobs place themseles in the working class (*Table 30*). A series of discriminant analyses were run dichotomizing occupational class at different points on the scale, with subjective class as the dependent variable, and the best split found was between A B C1 and C2 D (canonical correlation: $r = 0.34$), although a split between A B C1 C2 and D came not far behind ($r = 0.29$). Splitting the scale between the managerial and professional workers (A B) and a compound of manual and routine non-manual jobs (C1 C2 D) gave a very much poorer prediction of subjective class assignment ($r = 0.12$).

This suggests that in terms of subjective class identification, at least for the women in this sample, there is a clearly discernible divide between manual and non-manual workers; being in a professional, a managerial, *or a routine non-manual* job is a good predictor of the likelihood of claiming membership of the middle class. There is some indication, however, that while women in C2 jobs are less likely than those in the non-manual band to assign themselves to the middle class, they are more likely than those in semi- or unskilled jobs.

Class structure

When respondents were asked about the class placement of a set of occupations some of which were on the margins of this divide, however, if was found that a majority of respondents assigned all the marginal jobs to the working class. In *Table 46* the three routine non-manual jobs in the list which are usually associated with women (wages clerk, typist, and saleswoman) were seen as working-class jobs by over two-thirds of the sample. Splitting the sample by subjective class, however (see *Table 47*) we find that women who identified themselves as middle-class were more likely to see these jobs as middle-class than were subjectively working-class women. Thus of those who placed themselves in the middle class 46 per cent claimed 'wages clerk' for their own class, 44 per cent claimed 'typist', and 33 per cent claimed 'saleswoman' – the comparison figures for subjectively working-class women are 24 per cent, 15 per cent, and 15 per cent respectively.

This clearly raises the issue of what the determinants of class

Table 46   Assignment of selected occupations to classes (%)

occupation	class to which assigned	
	middle	working
Car mechanic	10.6	89.3
Foreman	20.7	79.3
Saleswoman	25.3	74.7
Typist	31.1	68.9
Wages clerk	36.5	63.5
Tobacconist	48.0	52.0

Table 47 Class assignment of 'female' jobs, by self-assigned class (%)

occupation	self-assigned class			
	middle		working	
		class assigned		
	middle	working	middle	working
Wages clerk	46.5	53.5	23.6	76.4
Typist	43.8	56.2	14.7	85.3
Saleswoman	33.5	66.5	14.5	85.5

are seen as being – what factors lead someone to identify themselves as belonging to a given class or to place another person in a given class – and also the question of what the class structure is into which people are being placed. These two questions would appear to be linked inextricably. In Chapter 4 we saw that background factors such as class of father and education, as well as own occupation and (for married women) husband's occupation explained some of the variance in class placement. However, for none of the groups did any one of these factors, or any combination, account for much more than 50 per cent of the variance. Some of the deficit in explanatory value will, of course, be due to measurement error and/or the crudity of the measures. The size of the shortfall, however, strongly suggests that factors other than those included in the models are also of importance.

Before we examine what are seen as the major determinants of class, we shall first look at the way in which the women in the sample saw the class structure into the categories of which they were prepared to place themselves and others. As we have said already, the majority of the respondents placed themselves without prompting in either the middle or the working class. When asked how many classes there are in Britain today, however, a majority said there were three or more, and this held true for those who saw themselves as working-class as well as for the middle-class respondents. However, there is some evidence that subjectively working-class women were more likely to see the social world as divided into just two classes than were the middle-class women (see *Table 48*). Marital status made no difference: a similar pattern emerged when single and

Table 48 All women: Number of classes perceived, by
self-assigned class

self-assigned class		number of classes		
		one	two	several
Middle	%	9	14	76
Working	%	14	33	53
Total	%	11	22	66

married women were analysed separately. Controlling for own
occupational class (for the women in employment), we found,
not surprisingly, that those most likely to say there are only two
classes in modern Britain were the women in manual jobs who
also defined themselves as working-class. Even here, however,
those who see two classes are still a minority – a quarter of the
single women and just under a third of the married ones.

As a crude indicator of the perceived relationship between
classes, respondents were asked to choose between two 'attitude items' one of which likened life to a ladder while the other
suggested that stability was more desirable; this may be seen as
tapping views about the possibility and desirability of social
mobility. Seventy per cent seemed to think that mobility was
both possible and desirable, as assessed from this item. Fewer
than 30 per cent thought that conflict between bosses and
workers was characteristic of modern Britain, in response to
another similar item. However, there were clear differences
between those who defined themselves as middle-class and
those who saw themselves as falling into the working class
(*Tables 49* and *50*). While nearly 80 per cent of the subjectively
middle-class women thought social mobility possible and
desirable, the figure drops to 58 per cent of the subjectively
working-class. A similar but less clear trend appears in the
responses on social conflict: of those who defined themselves as
middle-class only 24 per cent thought that conflict between
classes was prevalent in Britain today, and the figure rises to
over 36 per cent for the subjectively working-class respondents.
The pattern was very similar for married and single women,
although the former were slightly less likely than the latter to
see mobility as possible and desirable and rather more likely to

Table 49 All women: Views on mobility, by self-assigned class

self-assigned class		mobility possible and desirable	mobility not possible
Middle	%	78	22
Working	%	58	42
Total	%	70	30

Table 50 All women: Views of social conflict, by self-assigned class

self-assigned class		think conflict prevalent	think conflict not prevalent
Middle	%	24	76
Working	%	36	64
Total	%	29	71

identify class conflict. Those most likely to see modern Britain as an immobile, closed society were subjectively working-class women who were themselves in working-class jobs. The pattern with respect to class conflict is similar: women in manual employment were more likely to say there is conflict than women in non-manual employment, and among them the most likely to see conflict were those who saw themselves as working-class.

A considerable amount of agreement about the nature of the class structure in modern Britain appears to emerge. Over two-thirds of the women in the sample see British society as composed of three or more classes, with a relative absence of class conflict and with social mobility both possible and desirable. Those who diverge from this consensual image are mainly in manual occupations and are likely to define themselves as working-class, but they are a minority even of their group. It seems, then, that the boundaries of class are clearly perceived as far as self-assignment is concerned – women assign themselves 'correctly' to classes on the whole (though particular borderline occupations tend to be 'misclassified' in the abstract); on the other hand, more consensus than conflict is perceived in the relationship between classes. Self-defined class together with objective class (of own employment) does have some influence on how the social structure is perceived, but there is little evidence for a total divergence of view along class lines.

The determinants of class placement

As we have already seen, occupation is clearly an important determinant of subjective class placement and can be used to place others in social classes – although, as we have also seen, there is some ambiguity at the class boundaries. The results of previous research are by no means unambiguous on whether occupation is seen as the most important factor in class placement. Martin (1954) found it to be seen as the major determinant of class: manual work was most frequently associated with the working class (although some respondents included routine non-manual work in this category), and while the concept of a middle class was vague and ill-defined, occupation was mentioned by a majority of respondents as a determining factor. (The exceptions, less influenced by occupation, were subjectively middle-class respondents in objectively working-class occupations). Kahan *et al.* (1966) also found occupation to be the main criterion – mentioned by 61 per cent of respondents when describing the middle class and 74 per cent when describing the working class. However, both these studies found that factors such as income and education were also seen as relevant. Other surveys in Britain have also found that occupation is not necessarily the factor most frequently mentioned, especially when respondents are given a list of possible criteria from which to choose; *Table 51* summarizes the results of three such studies.

Runciman (1964), found some interesting differences when he compared self-rated and objective class. When asked the sort of person they meant when they talked about 'the working class' the largest single factor mentioned by nearly all groups was occupation, but only in the group who were both subjectively and objectively middle-class did a majority of respondents (65 per cent) refer to it; less than half of the subjectively and objectively working-class mentioned it, only a third of those in middle-class jobs who thought themselves working-class, and it was not the largest factor at all for those in working-class jobs who thought themselves middle-class. (Forty per cent of those in middle-class jobs who thought of themselves as working-

Table 51 Factors associated with class assignment in three surveys

	NOP (1972)	Reid (1978)	Townsend (1979)	
Sample	Men and women	Women	Men	Women
Factors listed	Way speak	Appearance and behaviour	Way of life	Way of life
	Where live	Family background	Job	Family
	Friends	Attitudes, beliefs, political views	Money	Money
	Job	Style of life	Family	Job
	School attended	Education	Education	Education
	Way spend money	Occupation		
	Dress	House/area lived in		
	Car ownership	Income		
		Prestige/standing in community		

class answered that when they said 'working class' they meant 'ordinary people'.) When asked what sort of person they meant by 'middle-class', the largest category for everyone except the subjectively middle-class manual workers was occupation – mentioned by about half of the middle-class sample and 43 per cent of the manual workers who identified themselves as working-class. The subjectively middle-class manual workers appeared to have no clear idea: 28 per cent of the responses, for instance, fall in the 'don't know/other' category, and 27 per cent in the category of 'personal criteria of approval'. *Table 52* summarizes the results.

Some of the differences in results may well be accounted for by differences in the type of sample or, more likely, differences in the way the questions were asked. Ideas may have changed over time: it is earlier research (e.g. Bott 1957; Martin 1954) which found that occupation was seen as the main factor, while more recent research has indicated that other factors may be at least as important, if not more so. There may also be confusion

Table 52 Factors associated with class assignment (Runciman 1966) by self-assigned class and own occupation (%)

sort of person meant by Occupation	middle-class				working-class			
	middle		working		middle		working	
Self-assigned class	M.C.	W.C.	M.C.	W.C.	M.C.	W.C.	M.C.	W.C.
Non-manual work	49	51	16	43				
Between top and bottom	11	3	14	6				
Personal criterion of approval	16	2	27	2				
M.C. style of life	10	10	12	10				
Rich	7	23	8	27				
Other/DK	12	19	28	21				
Manual work					65	28	34	42
Ordinary people					9	40	13	29
Poor					5	7	9	9
Personal criterion of approval					1	10	5	12
Personal criterion of disapproval					11	1	15	1
Other/DK					15	21	30	12

Note
Percentages based on respondents, not responses.

in the minds of respondents, as Platt (1971) has pointed out in a critical re-evaluation of some of the conclusions of the Affluent Worker Study (Goldthorpe *et al.* 1969), between *determinants* of class and *correlates* of class. For example, one of the main conclusions of the Affluent Worker Study was that the 'new' or 'privatized' manual worker saw the world through a 'money' model rather than the 'power' model of the traditional manual worker which divided the world sharply into a privileged and an exploited class. However, Platt shows that when asked to rank occupations, the income given for each occupation appeared to play no role in determining where the occupation was placed in the class hierarchy. She suggests that in fact the respondents may well have held an 'us and them' frame of reference, and that wealth or money may have been of significance only because it was *associated* with being one of 'them' – the rich.

To avoid the main dangers of multiple choice techniques, which involve at least partial predetermination of the possible range of responses by the researcher, the respondents in the People in Society Survey were asked first to describe in their own words the sort of person who falls into the class they had assigned themselves to, and then to describe the sort of person who falls into the other class. ('What sort of person do you mean when you talk about the middle/working class?') After this they were shown a list of categories culled from previous research and asked to say which they thought was the most important and the second most important in determining a person's class. (Two randomly ordered lists were used, alternately presented, to reduce order bias.) The items, shown in *Table 56* below, contain a mixture of what Hiller (1975a) would call 'objective criteria' and 'evaluative criteria'. The previous, open-ended questions were coded by interviewers after the interview, using a coding frame devised on the basis of pilot study results. Respondents gave as much detail as they wanted, and up to six characteristics could be coded, though in practice few respondents came up with more than one or two distinct categories. The coding frame is given in *Table 53*.

The responses given to the open-ended questions were wide ranging, but subjective/evaluative factors were mentioned more frequently than any single objective factor. In referring to the

Table 53   Coding frame for the People in Society open-ended questions on determinants of class, and frequency of responses (%)

sort of person meant by			
middle-class		*working-class*	
Professional/		Manual work	12.0
managerial	9.9	Manual and minor	
Non-manual	5.2	non-manual	6.4
Income/standard		Income/standard	
of living	16.4	of living	13.7
Education	12.1	Education	8.1
Style of life/		Style of life/	
attitude	36.0	attitude	28.3
Background	9.5	Background	6.6
		All who work	15.8
Miscellaneous	10.9	Miscellaneous	9.1

Note
% based on respondents, not responses.

middle class only 15 per cent mentioned occupation, while over 16 per cent mentioned standard of living/income, and 36 per cent mentioned style of life (see *Table 53*). Again in describing the working class, the most frequently used characteristic was style of life (28 per cent), and 16 per cent said that everyone who worked was working-class. Occupation was mentioned by 18 per cent – 6 per cent nominating manual plus routine non-manual jobs, and 12 per cent manual jobs alone.

When we look separately at how people characterized the *middle* class according to their own self-assigned class, the two groups produce similar patterns (*Table 54*). However, when we compare how subjectively middle-class or working-class people characterize the *working* class (*Table 55*) some differences do emerge. Style of life and attitude is the characteristic most frequently mentioned by the subjectively middle-class, but among the subjectively working-class the most frequent category is 'everyone who works'. While nearly 23 per cent of the subjectively middle class referred to occupation, only 13 per cent of the subjectively working class did so. We can see clearly, then, that occupation is not mentioned by the vast majority of respondents as a characteristic defining either the middle or the

Table 54 Responses to open-ended question on what is meant by middle-class, by self-assigned class (%)

response	self-assigned class	
	middle	working
Professional/managerial	9.3	10.8
Non-manual	5.2	4.8
Income/standard of living	14.5	19.1
Education	13.8	10.0
Style of life/attitude	36.1	35.7
Background	10.4	8.3
Miscellaneous	10.8	10.8

Note
% based on respondents, not responses.

Table 55 Responses to open-ended question on what is meant by working-class, by self-assigned class (%)

response	self-assigned class	
	middle	working
Manual work	14.7	8.6
Manual or routine non-manual	7.9	4.5
Income/standard of living	11.0	17.2
Education	11.2	4.1
Style of life	31.6	23.9
Background	7.1	5.9
All who work	7.1	27.3
Miscellaneous	9.5	8.5

Note
% based on respondents, not responses.

working class when they are asked to say freely what they mean by the two classes – though it assumes a subsidiary importance when subjectively middle-class women characterize the working class. The broad conclusion is in line with the more recent research cited above and suggests that there has indeed been a secular change, with occupation receding in recent years as a construct used to characterize classes.

However, there are some evident problems in the analysis of this question. First, it was open-ended, coded by inexperienced interviewers. Second, although advice was given (in a television programme and often in tutorials) on prompting in general, we do not know how much the interviewers prompted the respondents on this particular question, encouraging them to produce more material when they began to 'dry up'. (The point here is that the early responses, particularly if given without hesitation, probably represent salient and available factors in the respondents' consciousness, but that as they are encouraged to prolong the list they probably begin to draw on the 'cultural stock' of 'what people usually say about class', and the question becomes a test of knowledge of norms rather than a measure of salient individual constructs.) With hindsight one can see that it would have been useful to indicate which were the earlier responses, and perhaps to give some indication of which were produced without hesitation – but it is always easy to improve survey design with hindsight. Finally, we do not know the meaning of the terms for the individual respondents – what is implied by or entailed in what was said. It could be, for example, that occupation was mentioned infrequently because it was generally taken for granted as entailed by style of life, background, or income or indeed by the very wording of the question itself. As many of these problems are shared by other research studies, results such as these should always be treated with some caution.

However, when we look at the responses to the next question, where respondents were given a forced choice on a pre-set list of characteristics, we find that occupation is still not seen as the major determinant or even the second most important one (see *Table 56*). The answers from both subjectively middle-class and subjectively working-class respondents are spread across all the criteria, but middle-class people are more likely to select 'how people live' than working-class ones, while the working class are more likely to pick 'wealth and property' than the subjectively middle class. Given that respondents pick two criteria it is interesting and sometimes illuminating to see how the choices are associated. For example, just looking at the most frequently chosen criteria, a cluster of 'how people live', 'occupation', 'education', and 'background' is quite apparent; those who pick one as first choice are quite likely to pick one of the three others as second. ('Manner' is also a quite likely second choice if 'how people live' is the first response.) Sub-

Table 56 Association between determinants of class chosen in response to the forced choice question, by self-assigned class

	how live	education	wealth	manner	income	background	power	other	total
self-assigned class: middle									
Occupation	7	11	3	2	2	4	1	0.1	31.6
How people live		8	4	8	3	8	0.3	—	40.0
Education			3	3	1	12	0.5	—	39.2
Wealth and property				1	2	5	1	—	20.5
Manner					0.1	3	—	—	17.9
Income						1	0.5	—	11.0
Background							0.5	—	33.6
Power								0.2	4.2
Other									
self-assigned class: working									
Occupation	5	6	6	1	4	4	0.5	—	25.7
How people live		4	6	4	3	5	0.6	—	27.1
Education			6	5	4	8	0.6	—	32.3
Wealth and property				0.6	6	10	3	0.1	37.3
Manner					0.6	2	0.1	—	12.6
Income						5	0.4	—	22.7
Background							0.6	0.1	34.3
Power								—	5.4
Other									

Notes
1 The figures in the tables are percentages of the appropriate self-assigned class.
2 The 'total' column records the percentage who picked a given item at all, whether on first or second choice.

jectively working-class respondents who selected 'wealth and property' as their main criterion most frequently selected background as their second, but 'occupation', 'how people live', 'education', or 'income' were also popular choices. Those who selected 'background tended to combine it with 'manner' or 'wealth or property' or 'income'. Those who selected education tended to combine it with manner or with background, and those who selected occupation to combine it with education or income.

This confused picture, with few clear patterns, is rendered if anything more confused still if we look at the full set of combinations of first and second choices. Virtually every combination was selected by both subjectively middle-class and subjectively working-class women, by at least a few respondents, and no particular combination was exceptionally popular. For middle-class women the most popular combinations were education and background (selected by 11.6 per cent), and occupation and education (11.2 per cent). The only combination selected by more than 10 per cent of the working-class respondents was wealth/property with background, chosen by 10.2 per cent.

Rather clearer patterns do begin to emerge if we group the individual characteristics into 'subjective' criteria (style of life, manner), 'objective status' criteria (occupation, education, income, background) and 'objective proletarian' criteria (wealth/property, power) – see *Table 57*. We can see then that a majority of respondents used at least some element of objective status in determining social class. Over a third of the subjectively middle-class and nearly a third of the working-class use *only* objective status criteria. A very small minority use objective proletarian criteria alone – about 1 per cent of the middle-class and almost 3 per cent of the working-class – but nearly a third of subjectively working-class respondents and a sixth of middle-class ones used objective proletarian criteria in combination with objective status ones. Thus in total over half of the women, irrespective of subjective class, determine class on the basis of objective criteria. In addition nearly 40 per cent of the middle-class and nearly 30 per cent of the working-class offer a mix of objective and subjective criteria; generally the mixture involves objective status criteria – objective proletarian criteria are included in it by

Table 57   Responses to forced choice question on determinants of class, summarized according to type, by self-assigned class (%)

type	self-assigned class	
	middle	working
Objective status	34.6	30.4
Objective proletarian	1.4	2.8
Subjective	8.3	3.7
Objective status plus proletarian	15.6	32.3
Objective status plus subjective	32.1	20.1
Objective proletarian plus subjective	6.4	7.6

Note
For definition of categories, see text.

less than 8 per cent of either group. In conclusion we can say that of the middle-class women, over 80 per cent determine class by reference at least in part to objective status criteria, nearly 50 per cent by reference at least in part to subjective criteria, and 23 per cent by reference at least in part to objective proletarian criteria. For subjectively working-class women, nearly 85 per cent refer at least in part to objective status criteria, but over 40 per cent refer at least in part to objective proletarian criteria, and only 30 per cent cite subjective criteria. Thus one can see a measure of broad agreement but a difference in the use of the categories 'wealth/property' and 'power'. (There were no obvious differences by marital or employment status.)

However, a note of caution needs to be introduced. We have categorized occupation, education, income, and background as objective status criteria, and power, wealth, and property as objective proletarian criteria (following the main lines of existing class theory) and manner and how people live as subjective criteria. Some of these allocations are not beyond dispute. 'Background', for instance, might be seen as an objectively proletarian criterion – 'he comes from the class in power' – but on balance we expect it to be used more broadly than this and thus have classified it under 'status'. However, in general this alerts us to the problem that *we do not know what people meant when they picked one of these factors*. Wealth and property, for instance, could be a power-marker – 'she comes from a rich industrial family' – or it could be a status marker – 'he owns his own home'. Education, even, is not without doubt an objective factor – 'he's an educated sort of chap' is not *necessarily* saying anything very different from 'manner' or 'style of life/attitude'. This is the classic problem of forced choice arrays: we put our own interpretation on the responses, and this is not necessarily a reflection of the respondent's interpretation.

We might perhaps cast a little light on what the categories meant to the respondents by looking at what they said in answer to the preceding open-ended questions. *Tables 58* and *59* show their responses to the questions 'What kind of person do you mean when you talk about' the middle class and the working class, against whether particular items were picked as first *or* second choice on the forced-choice questions. The description above of 'how people live' and 'manner' as subjective criteria seems partially validated by this comparison: whichever class is being described, people who picked these items were more likely to mention style of life or income/standard of living than other categories of response on the open-ended questions. Elsewhere the interpretation is less clear. On the 'objective proletarian' items the most frequent category mentioned on the earlier questions was also 'style of life'. On the 'objective status' items we find that occupation is most frequently paired with style of life again, followed by education and occupation; education is paired with style of life, occupation, and income/standard of living; income is paired with style, with income/standard of living and (more when describing the working class) with occupation. Some items are 'correlated' on the two measures – for example, occupation is fairly often mentioned spontaneously by those who also chose it from the list, and similarly with education. Others, however, are not: people who chose background from the list mentioned it quite often when talking about the middle class, but not so often when talking about the working class. Thus there is some evidence that we have clustered the categories correctly, but it is diluted by an overall preponderance of 'style of life' responses on the open-ended questions and by some indication that the two questions are provoking rather different sorts of responses and thus seeming to give unstable or even unreliable measurement. The best conclusion from the figures might be that the

Table 58 Association of items named as descriptive of the middle class with forced-choice selection of determinants of class

determinants (on first or second choice)		prof./manag. occupation	non-manual occupation	descriptive item income	education	style of life	background	misc.
Occupation	%	17	7	13	18	30	6	9
How people live	%	7	4	18	10	36	12	13
Education	%	11	5	14	16	36	8	10
Wealth and property	%	7	4	18	10	40	9	10
Manner	%	9	4	11	10	46	8	13
Income	%	8	7	31	7	34	4	8
Background	%	10	5	14	10	35	15	11
Power	%	4	6	12	10	36	12	20

Table 59 Association of items named as descriptive of the working class with forced-choice selection of determinants of class

determinants (on first or second choice)		manual work	manual and routine non-manual	income	descriptive items				
					education	style of life	background	all who work	misc.
Occupation	%	18	10	10	11	26	5	12	10
How people live	%	10	5	15	6	32	7	15	10
Education	%	13	7	15	11	27	8	12	7
Wealth and property	%	10	5	14	8	31	4	19	8
Manner	%	11	8	12	3	29	5	18	15
Income	%	8	5	23	6	26	6	18	8
Background	%	12	6	11	8	27	9	20	8
Power	%	8	4	9	6	31	8	20	13

results of detailed analysis should be treated with considerable caution, and that Platt (1971) is right to point to a confusion in popular consciousness between what *determines* or *defines* a class position and what generally correlates with or goes along with it: the middle class may enjoy a good 'style of life', but this is as likely to be seen as a *consequence* of being middle-class than as what makes the person middle-class in the first place.

What we *can* conclude, however, is that occupation is not seen as a major determinant of class by the women in this sample, despite the high correlation they display between objective occupational class and subjective class alignment. They are more concerned with status factors as a whole (among which occupation is only one) and with subjective factors, which might tend perhaps to suggest that the majority see society more in terms of a continuous hierarchy than in terms of bounded classes. This contention would be supported by the fact that a majority did not see classes as in conflict and thought social mobility both desirable and possible, and by the large number of times 'style of life' was mentioned as associated with class membership in the open-ended questions.

Voting behaviour

Given this overall appearance of consensus about the class structure (albeit with women who consider themselves working-class rather more likely to display some element of proletarian imagery), we are in a position to turn to another possible aspect of class identification – voting behaviour. Until recently a strong relationship has been assumed by political scientists between class and voting behaviour – the Labour Party being seen as a party of the working class and the Conservatives as a middle-class party. Indeed, those who did not vote for the party that was seen as representing their class interests tended to be considered 'deviants', and considerable research was undertaken in the 1950s and 1960s into why, in particular, people in manual occupations voted for the Conservative Party.

The Party Identification theory argues that the political parties reflect class interests and receive their support mainly from the class they 'represent'. More broadly, various aspects of the social structure such as age, housing, union membership, occupational sector, and social class constitute the basis of voting behaviour by defining groups likely to vote in particular ways. Voting is seen as influenced by group membership as well as by the expressed attitudes of parents, friends, and work-mates, and is seen in part as an act of solidarity with one's social group. Thus, for example, working-class people vote Labour because of class solidarity, because Labour is seen as 'their' party representing their interests in general (and because they always have voted Labour, and their parents before them), not just because Labour is seen consciously as representing their interests on particular issues. In this view the recent decline in Labour Party support from the working class can be explained in terms of an erosion of its demographic class basis – that is, for example, a decline in the number of manual workers living in council houses, etc. (see e.g. Crewe 1979), who would be its natural supporters.

An alternative explanation for voting behaviour, the Instrumental Theory, has been put forward more recently (Himmelweit, Humphreys, and Jaeger 1981). Based on the ideas of Downs (1957), this theory argues that voting is not just a matter of group identification, but very much a question of rational choices being made between the programmes which the parties put forward: voters aiming to maximize their own interests choose between the packages of policies on offer. The decline in class solidarity would then have to be interpreted as a growing failure by the political parties to sell themselves and their policies as in the interests of those on whose votes they used to rely.

However, Heath, Jowell, and Curtice (1985) argue that the antithesis between these two theories is more apparent than real. They suggest that voters have never supported parties out of blind loyalty, on the one hand, and on the other that there is still some element of class allegiance in current voting behaviour. They demonstrate that the Labour Party's social base has indeed declined, while the salaried classes have grown. However, they found that the Labour vote had fallen more than would be expected from the decline in its social base, and they argue that this is the result of fluctuations in political influence and reflects the changing confidence in political parties. Their analysis of the 1983 general election confirms a class base for each of the three main political parties. Fifty-five per cent of Labour voters were working-class, and 49 per cent of the working class voted Labour, while 71 per cent of Conservative voters were middle-class, and 57 per cent of the middle class voted Conservative. The Alliance also seems to be a party of the middle class; 63 per cent of its support came from the middle classes, and 25 per cent of the middle classes voted for it (see *Table 60*). It seems, then, that there is still a relationship between class and voting behaviour, though not as strong a relationship as may have been discernible in the past.

It has also been argued that women's political behaviour is different from that of men, although the arguments have often been contradictory in nature and not well sustained by the empirical evidence. (For a fuller discussion see Randall 1982; Siltanen and Stanworth 1984). Thus it has been suggested that women are less likely to vote at all than men, and this is used to argue that women are less interested in politics than men. However, when allowance is made for age, given that older people are less likely to vote than younger ones and women survive on average to greater age, the apparent difference virtually disappears (Crewe *et al.* 1977: 59; Lansing 1977; Rose 1976). Women, it is often argued, are influenced in their voting behaviour by their husbands (see e.g. Lazarsfeld, Berelson and Gaudet 1968). However, the bulk of the evidence suggests

Table 60 Class and voting in the 1983 general election (%)

source of support	Conservative	Labour	Alliance	others
Professional and managerial	34	14	35	24
Routine non-manual	25	21	26	37
Petty bourgeoisie	12	3	5	2
Foremen and technicians	8	6	7	5
Working class	21	55	26	32
party choice by class				
Professional and managerial	54	14	31	1
Routine non-manual	46	25	25	2
Petty bourgeoisie	71	12	17	—
Foremen and technicians	48	26	25	1
Working class	30	49	20	1

Reprinted with permission from Heath, A., Jowell, R., and Curtice, J. *How Britain Votes*, pp. 20–1, copyright 1985, Pergamon Books Ltd.

mutual influence (e.g. Maccoby, Matthews, and Morton *et al.* 1954; Jennings and Niemi 1974; Prandy 1986; Weiner, 1978). Finally, women are said to be more conservative than men – that is, more likely to vote for the Conservative Party (e.g. Blondel 1965). A number of theories have been put forward to account for this. Lane (1959) has argued that it occurs because 'being a woman' is incompatible with 'being a socialist' – a confusion of sex-roles. Religion has frequently been seen as a key factor; women are more religious than men and the Church of England has been identified with the Conservative Party. Employment status has also been seen as a major explanatory factor (e.g. Aitkin and Kahan 1974). It is argued that the work experiences of manual workers are a key factor in their Labour voting, whether they be men or women; Taylor's survey in the 1970s of the party identification of working-class men and women found that employed men and women were both likely to identify with Labour but that full-time housewives showed a greater likelihood of identifying with the Conservative Party (though even among the housewives Labour support was stronger than Conservative support).

However, the differences between the voting behaviour of men and women in Britain since 1945 have always been small (Goot and Reid 1975). Indeed, in some general elections women have tended to prefer the Labour to the Conservative Party – in 1945, for instance (Durant 1966) and in 1964 (Butler and King 1965). Furthermore, in both the 1979 and the 1983 General Elections more men than women have voted Conservative; in 1979 46 per cent of men voted Conservative and 45 per cent of women, and in 1983 the figures were 46 per cent and 44 per cent.

Political scientists have not in general been concerned with women's political behaviour; when women have been included in surveys their class has been determined by that of their (male) head of household, and the interest has focused on differences between the genders rather than on within-gender differences between women. It has generally been assumed that women are less interested in political issues than men because their main interest lies in the private sphere, and that their major concern is with moral rather than political issues. However, this division between a public and a private sphere is itself a political issue, and to say that a concern with working conditions, education, maternity leave, abortion, and the like displays an interest in moral rather than political issues is to make a very loaded value judgement (see Siltanen and Stanworth 1984). It may well be that women's experiences are different from men's and there- fore determine their voting behaviour differently. In times of high inflation, for example, women may not benefit from their husbands' increased wages. Women may be more affected than men by cuts in public spending (or more aware of the result) in such areas as education, health, and the implementation of community care policies. It has been ably argued by Dorothy Smith (1979) that women live less in the 'abstract mode' of conceptual argument and more in the concrete reality in which the arguments are grounded – indeed, that women function to isolate men from this concrete reality – and areas such as schooling and health provision illustrate her point very well; men may have theories on education and health care, but it is women who pick up the children from school and take them to the doctor. Working hours, the provision of nurseries, ante- natal provision, and the availability of abortions may also be more important to women, who retain the major responsibility for child care. All these are political issues and may influence how women vote; to ignore them is to ignore the basis on which women may make political choices – including the decision not to vote. Finally, if women *are* less interested in politics than men (although the empirical evidence for this is not strong), this may be because they feel they have little chance of influencing what happens, not only as a realistic appraisal of the situation but also because politics and what is seen as political are dominated by men.

Heath, Jowell, and Curtice included both men and women in their study of the 1983 general election, classified according to their own occupation if they were in work. (Full-time house- wives were classified by occupation of head of household.) As their survey used random sampling techniques its results are more likely to be representative of the population than ours – see Chapter 2. (Note, however, as was argued there, that the non-representative nature of the sample does not invalidate conclusions about the nature of particular groups of women and the way that groups may differ; the only thing it precludes is straightforward generalization from sample percentages to percentages in the population.) Looking briefly at how men and women voted in 1983, *Table 61* gives the distribution of votes by gender and occupational class. (An important factor to bear in mind when comparing female voting patterns with male ones is the differential distribution of men and women across the occupational classes. In the Heath, Jowell, and Curtice survey the distribution was as would be expected: a concentration of women in routine non-manual occupations, with men more concentrated in professional/managerial and manual occupations.) The main point that emerges in *Table 61* is the low level of support for the Labour Party compared with preceding elections. Gender differences are small, the main one being that women in the 'foremen and technicians' category are more likely to vote Labour than their male colleagues, whose support goes more to the Alliance. The reverse is true for manual workers, with women more likely to support the Alliance and men to vote Labour. Level of support for the Conservatives does not differ by gender.

These data are presented to demonstrate that the differences in political party preference between men and women were virtually non-existent in 1983, and that class differences appear to be a more important factor. (It may well be, of course, that

Table 61　Class, gender, and voting in the 1983 general election

			Conservative	Labour	Alliance	others
Professional and	women	%	54	14	30	2
managerial	men	%	54	14	31	1
Routine non-manual	women	%	45	26	27	2
	men	%	48	23	27	2
Petty bourgeoisie	women	%	72	11	17	—
	men	%	70	13	16	1
Foremen and	women	%	48	30	21	—
technicians	men	%	48	24	26	1
Working class	women	%	29	46	24	1
	men	%	30	51	17	2
TOTAL	women	%	44	28	27	1
	men	%	46	30	24	1

Reprinted with permission from Heath, A., Jowell, R., and Curtice, J. *How Britain Votes*, p. 24, copyright 1985, Pergamon Books Ltd.

some of the apparent class differences are in fact a product of classifying full-time housewives by their husbands' occupations.) However, it should not be assumed that these data or any other survey taken at a particular time can be generalized to the current population to give any reasonable indication of current voting preferences. At the time of writing (August 1986) the opinion polls indicate strong support for the Labour Party and less for Conservatives or the Alliance. This situation in turn can and probably will change. Furthermore, the emergence of the Alliance as a third party with strong electoral support makes comparison with previous elections difficult. Britain appears to have changed from an effective two-party system to a three-party one. (Voting in Northern Ireland, however, is very different from what happens on the mainland and always has been, and Scotland and Wales have nationalist parties whose fortunes fluctuate and who gain or lose support across the political spectrum.)

The People in Society Survey does not enable us to tackle most of the issues vital to an understanding of women's political behaviour and the differences between women in their voting. However, it does allow us to look at party identification (a more realistic indicator of political preference than how someone happens to have voted at the last general election), and to analyse this by such factors as age, occupation, education, subjective social class, etc. This will at least let us begin the task of examining within-gender differences between women rather than restricting the analysis to how women differ from men, and to speculate on the relationship of this form of (arguably) class action to women's class identification.

The data used in this analysis were collected in March/April of each year from 1981 to 1984. An analysis by year of collection showed fluctuation in party preference interpretable in the light of contemporary events, despite the fact that respondents were asked not for whom they had last voted but who they generally supported or voted for at general elections. Also a not insubstantial proportion of the sample (about 14 per cent) said that their support varied or they did not support any particular party. In addition, between 4 and 5 per cent of the female sample chose a party other than one of the three main ones. In terms of support for the three major parties over all the years of data, a third of the women identified with the Labour Party, slightly fewer with the Conservatives, and about 16 per cent with the Liberal/SDP Alliance. Regional variations were as would be expected: stronger support for the Conservatives in the South and for Labour in the North; Alliance support was spread across the country but was strongest in the South-West. There is a clear relationship between subjective social class and party preference. The women who voted Labour included over half of those who assigned themselves to the working class, but only 20 per cent of those who assigned themselves to the middle class; nearly two-thirds of the support for the Labour Party comes from women who consider themselves working-class, in this sample. Conversely, about 42 per cent of the subjectively middle-class women voted Conservative, compared with about 18 per cent of those who consider themselves working-class, and over three-quarters of the Conservative support comes from middle-class women. The Alliance is supported by about 20 per cent of subjectively middle-class women and about 12 per cent of working-class women; 70 per cent of its support comes from the middle class and 30 per cent from the working class.

A similar relationship between class and party preference can be seen using head of household's class rather than subjective self-assignment as the measure of class. We can see (*Table 63*)

Table 62   Women's party preference by self-assigned class in the People in Society survey

source of support		self-assigned class	
		middle	working
Labour	%	34	66
Conservative	%	76	24
Alliance	%	70	30
Other	%	67	33
Various/none	%	54	46
party preference		%	%
Labour		20	52
Conservative		42	18
Alliance		20	12
Other		5	4
Various/none		13	15

Table 63 Women's party preference by class of head of household

source of support		A	B	C1	C2	D	E
				head of household's class			
Labour	%	5	22	10	30	23	9
Conservative	%	13	32	22	22	8	3
Alliance	%	7	35	19	22	11	6
Others	%	13	32	18	21	11	4
Various/none	%	6	26	18	32	16	2
party preference		%	%	%	%	%	%
Labour		21	26	21	38	51	54
Conservative		38	48	41	27	18	19
Alliance		14	20	18	14	13	17
Others		7	5	5	4	3	3
Various/none		10	13	15	17	15	6

that over 50 per cent of Labour Party support came from people classified as working-class by head of household's job (plus a further 9 per cent where head of household was unemployed or retired); less than 40 per cent is attributable to women classified as middle-class on head of household's occupation. The strongest support came from women whose head of household was in a semi- or unskilled manual job (51 per cent); only 38 per cent of those whose head of household was in a skilled manual job voted Labour. Father's class also seems to influence Labour voting (*Table 64*); again, over half of those whose father was in a semi- or unskilled job voted Labour, and 37 per cent of women with fathers in skilled manual work. Own occupation, for those who were in work, is another correlated variable (*Table 65*); again, over 50 per cent of the semi- and unskilled voted Labour, and 35 per cent of the skilled.

Conservative Party support comes, as would be expected, from women with non-manual connections; women whose head of household is in a non-manual job, and daughters of middle-class fathers, are more likely to support the Conservative Party than any other. However, among economically active women those in A or C1 are more likely to support the Conservative Party while those in B are more likely to vote Labour. This is an unexpected break in pattern, and may be an

Table 64 Women's party preference by father's class

source of support		A	B	father's class C1	C2	D	E
Labour	%	6	14	13	40	25	2
Conservative	%	16	22	22	31	8	<1
Alliance	%	11	20	19	34	13	2
Others	%	8	24	18	34	12	2
Various/none	%	9	18	11	43	17	1
party preference		%	%	%	%	%	%
Labour		20	25	26	37	52	54
Conservative		47	38	41	27	17	5
Alliance		17	17	18	15	13	22
Others		4	6	5	4	3	8
Various/none		12	13	9	16	15	11

Table 65 Women's party preference by own occupation

source of support		A	B	own occupation C1	C2	D	E
Labour	%	1	18	17	12	36	15
Conservative	%	2	16	44	8	16	13
Alliance	%	1	21	40	13	12	13
Others	%	1	27	31	11	18	12
Various/none	%	2	18	30	17	24	9
party preference		%	%	%	%	%	%
Labour		26	32	17	35	52	38
Conservative		43	28	44	22	22	31
Alliance		14	19	21	18	8	17
Others		2	7	4	4	4	4
Various/none		14	14	13	20	15	10

Note
'Class' E is made up mostly of full-time housewives.

artefact of quota sampling. It seems likely, given the nature of
the interviewers (Open University students) that more women
than would be typical of the general population were sampled
from among semi-professional workers in the public sector –
particularly teachers. Recent research (Crewe 1979) has suggested that employment in the public sector may be associated
with a tendency to vote Labour rather than Conservative.

Alliance support comes in this sample from women with middle-class or skilled manual connections. In fact, in terms of class of origin 34 per cent of female support for the Alliance comes from daughters of skilled manual workers, and 35 per cent comes from women whose head of household is employed in a semi-professional or lower managerial position. However, in terms of own occupation the support for the Alliance is found mainly among those in routine non-manual occupations.

What these figures confirm is that the Conservatives are a middle-class party and that Labour is a working-class party. The Alliance also seems to attract votes from the middle class. However, there is cross-class voting even when we look at the relationship between *subjective* class and voting behaviour. Some women who see themselves as middle-class do vote Labour none the less – though only 20 per cent of them. A similar proportion (*c.* 18 per cent) of those who place themselves in the working class vote Conservative. More of those who place themselves in the middle class vote for the Alliance than of those who place themselves in the working class (20 per cent compared with 12 per cent).

There also seems to be a relationship between party identification and education, but it is not as straightforward as might be expected. On both the measures of educational level (years of post-compulsory schooling and qualifications achieved) there seems to be a tendency for the better educated to favour the Alliance – 23 per cent of those with post-'A' level qualifications as compared with 13 per cent of the others, and 23 per cent of those who stayed on at school for 2+ years after the minimum leaving age, compared with 18 per cent of those who stayed on only one year and 12 per cent of those who left at the minimum age. (In fact Heath *et al.* have argued that the Alliance is the party of the intelligentsia.) There is also an association between Labour voting and having left school at the minimum age, and between staying on at school and voting Conservative, but those who stayed on for 2+ years seem less strong in their support than those who stayed on for only one year. The relationship with qualifications achieved is less clear.

There appears to be no strong clear relationship between ageing and party preference. The age-bands in which support for the Conservatives was strongest were 35–45 and 55+, while

Table 66   Party preference and educational level in women

source of support		years of post-compulsory schooling			educational qualifications	
		None	1	2+	less than 'A' level	'A' level or higher
Labour	%	62	6	31	75	25
Conservative	%	47	13	40	71	29
Alliance	%	35	11	54	56	44
Others	%	44	9	48	52	48
Various/none	%	50	11	39	68	32
party preference		%	%	%	%	%
Labour		41	20	26	38	28
Conservative		29	42	32	31	28
Alliance		12	18	23	13	23
Others		4	4	6	4	7
Various/none		14	16	14	14	15

support for Labour was strongest among those aged 25–34, 45–54 and 65+. There does not seem, therefore, to be any tendency for women to become more conservative as they get older, though there may be a discernible tendency for older people to choose one or other of the two main parties rather than choosing the Alliance or some other party or expressing no particular preference.

Finally we looked at the relationship between employment status and party identification for married women – it having been argued that women who are full-time housewives are less likely to vote Labour as they do not directly experience the work situation. However, we found no evidence to support this argument. Employed women were slightly but not significantly more likely to vote Labour than full-time housewives (35 per cent compared with 33 per cent), but those who worked part-time were more likely to vote Labour (38 per cent) than those who worked full-time. The difference in Conservative support between married working women and full-time housewives was also slight; 32 per cent of employed women and 34 per cent of housewives supported the Conservative Party.

A series of multiple regression analyses was run to try to determine what would predict support for the Conservative

Table 67 Party preference in women and age

source of support		18–24	25–34	age 35–44	45–54	55–64	65+
Labour	%	15	33	18	16	11	6
Conservative	%	16	29	24	12	13	6
Alliance	%	18	32	28	13	8	3
Others	%	12	39	26	15	8	—
Various/none	%	30	35	17	8	5	4
party preference		%	%	%	%	%	%
Labour		29	35	28	40	36	41
Conservative		29	30	35	29	42	37
Alliance		17	15	21	17	12	10
Others		3	6	5	5	4	—
Various/none		21	15	10	9	6	12

Party, or support for Labour. For women as a whole the two main predictors, for either party, were subjective social class and father's class, but father's class contributed very little to the prediction of Labour voting; educational qualifications and head of household's occupation also made small but significant contributions to the prediction of Conservative voting. Looking at full-time housewives, the same variables emerge in the analysis, but class of husband makes a rather larger contribution (though still less than the variance explained by subjective class). For employed married women, class of father appears to be important, though subjective class still enters the equation, and own class and educational variables make a significant contribution. (Husband's class did not enter the equation.) For single women, subjective class was the *only* predictor of Labour preference, and the first (followed by father's class and educational qualifications) of Conservative preference. Three points of interest emerge from these analyses. First, very little of the variance was explained – seldom much more than 10 per cent; class may predict voting, but it is clearly very far from sufficient as an explanation of it. Second, the major predictor was *subjective* social class, in almost all the analyses. Third, husband's class would not appear on the surface to be much of an influence on voting. (However, this conclusion is not sustainable from these data, as we do not know how the *husbands* voted; 'cross-class' voting is no less common among men than women.)

We see, then, that there is some relationship between subjective class and party identification. We have also seen that subjective class is influenced by objective class, among other factors, and that the two are associated with views on the social structure and on the determinants of class. We have not found a strong correlation between class alignment and class action, in so far as party preference is a measure of the latter, but there does seem to be a substantial consensus about the kind of social world we live in, as measured by each of the items in the survey which we have considered in this chapter. The task of the next chapter is to try to relate these disparate items together in a more holistic picture – to see whether the women in the sample really do have a single overall picture of society, or whether interpretable differences can be discerned.

6 Images of society

In this chapter we attempt to build on the picture of the social stratification system within which women work that we began to develop in the last chapter. What we are looking at is what previous research has referred to as social class imagery – the complex mental map within which people make sense of the social structure which frames their day-to-day lives.

Most writers on social stratification have given some consideration to social actors' consciousness of social class. There is obviously a strong link between class orientation and class action, and for political, theoretical, and methodological reasons research in this area has tended to concentrate on male manual workers – as the class whose potential action is of most interest, as the class whose *lack* of action has most to be explained, and as a conveniently remote focus for predominantly middle-class researchers. Less research has been carried out on the class imagery of men in non-manual occupations, and even less on women. The lack of research on women is partly, as we have seen, because women have been considered marginal to the workplace (and by implication to political action) and partly because women have been seen as part of 'the household', placed by their husband's occupation and presumably sharing his imagery (though there has been a tendency, as we saw in Chapter 5, to regard women as more conservative than men and more interested in moral than in political issues). It is not self-evident, however, nor suggested by available evidence that married women's attitudes and self-location are necessarily well predicted by those of their husbands; nor is it by any means the case that all women are married. The evidence for the 'innate' conservatism of women and their disinclination towards political issues would also seem either to be lacking or to be based on a distinctly partisan definition of what constitutes a political issue. It seems worthwhile, therefore, to explore women's imagery in its own right, in parallel to the research on men, to see whether gender differences can be detected and in general how the understudied 51 per cent of the population understand their social world.

Social imagery research on males

In previous research on stratification and class imagery, occupation had been taken as a good proxy or summary indicator of objective social and economic differences between people. Research has been concerned to elicit people's recognition of the existence of social classes, their perception of the class structure and whether they see classes in terms of conflict or harmony. The results of such research are generally analysed in terms of the relationship between objective social class (as determined by occupation) and subjective perceptions, either for individuals or for whole groups. An attempt is made to establish what connections exist between objective social class and subjective social class – i.e. how people actually experience inequalities of income, unequal educational opportunities, and so on. While it is recognized that there may be no simple link between objective and subjective aspects of stratification, nevertheless it is argued that while an individual's ideas may be wrong or invalid they are still likely to have real consequences, and thus that it is important to discover what individuals really think and feel.

Class imagery research, then, is concerned with exploring the detailed meaning of class identification and the complex mental representations which underlie it – the model of the class structure within which the individual operates. This goes beyond the type of analysis we have undertaken in Chapters 4 and 5, which was concerned with class identification and classification; we are concerned now with the important question of what people understand by class and their own class location. Class identification is itself a problematic concept and may conceal many different processes or meanings: for example, a manual worker claiming membership of the middle class may mean something very different in so doing from non-manual workers who claim middle-class status. It is therefore necessary to investigate an individual's overall conception of the class structure of society, while at the same time recognizing that class images are not as logical or coherent in reality as the ideal types constructed by social scientists. For example, Roberts *et al.* (1977) found thirty white-collar workers in their sample who could be described as having traditional proletarian class imagery, but nearly two-thirds of them had voted Conservative at the last general election!

It is also recognized that people experiencing the same objective situations may respond to them differently – that is, the same objective reality may create different subjective responses. Bott (1957) argues that these differences are connected with the social relationships in which individuals are involved: class ideologies result from experience of the interacting norms of the primary group. Thus individuals in close-knit working-class communities have a 'power model' (that is, an 'us and them' view of class, with the interests of the working class and 'them' in conflict). Conversely, those experiencing more open types of social network have a 'prestige model' of class, seeing themselves in the middle of a hierarchy and wanting upward mobility. Mackenzie (1975) argues that the major factor shaping social imagery is the work situation (see also Lockwood 1958). Mackenzie suggests that male workers who undertake fragmented, routinized manual work, are controlled by impersonal bureaucratic authority relationships and work in circumstances where group solidarity and conformity are stressed and where there is little possibility of social mobility would tend towards a working-class social imagery. Middle-class social imagery is held by male workers who do non-manual work which is varied and creative, who have control over other workers and/or have a personal, face-to-face relationship with those in authority over them; here individuality is stressed, social mobility is seen as desirable and possible, and either highly specialized technology or virtually no technology at all is utilized. In contrast, Parkin (1972) and Ossowski (1963) both argue that meaning systems serve an ideological function and suggest that putting forward appropriate images of society is a stratagem that dominant classes can use to legitimate and thereby consolidate their position. In other words, class imagery may be seen as a cause or maintaining factor rather than a consequence of social and workplace divisions.

However class images may be formed and sustained, research

has demonstrated that most men do have a social imagery and that social imagery does help to explain how objective features of the class structure are sustained – although there is debate over the extent to which consistent and coherent images of society can be identified. On the one hand, Willener (1957) and with some reservations Goldthorpe (1970) argue that coherent, consistent images can be identified; on the other, Blackburn and Mann (1975) argue that they cannot. Other researchers (e.g. Hiller 1975a; Cousins and Brown 1975; Roberts *et al.* 1977) suggest a midway position – that is, that there are images of society but that these are fragmentary within classes and that some respondents cannot be classified as holding an identifiable and coherent typification of the social structure. In the various attempts which have been made to develop a taxonomy of respondents' images of society the resulting numbers of class models elicited have varied widely. Bott (1957) found four distinct models, Roberts *et al.* (1977) found five, and Hiller (1975b) identified eleven. Most surveys have also found a significant number of respondents who claim to have no image of class: Goldthorpe and Hope found 26 per cent, for instance, and Roberts *et al.* found 17 per cent. Research also suggests that there is considerable overlap in the social imagery of manual and non-manual workers (Hiller 1975a; Roberts *et al.* 1977). Studies have also found little evidence to support the view that either manual or non-manual workers consider that there is considerable conflict in modern Britain, although Labour voters tend to see more than others (Moorhouse 1976). It could also be argued that researchers tend to force data into pre-existing categories – ideal types – rather than to consider them as valid data in their own right (see e.g. Hiller 1975a).

Research has been designed, implicitly or explicitly, to test theoretical 'ideal types' of social imagery. Lockwood's three ideal types of the working class, which attempt to relate views on class structure to the situation at work and in the community, are frequently cited. Lockwood suggests that one type within the working class is the traditional proletarian worker who lives and works in the same community and who holds a power model of class (two main classes in conflict). (Note, however, as Westergaard (1975) has argued, that there is no reason why the 'power/conflict' model should be restricted to those who see only two classes. It is quite possible to recognize the existence of a middle class but still hold to a conflict model of society.) Cousins and Brown (1970, 1975) found that only a third of the shipbuilders they studied held this model, others mentioning as many as six classes and the majority seeing class differences in terms of money, possessions, and so on. Nevertheless, 80 per cent of their respondents did see themselves at the lower end of a class hierarchy, and 46 per cent referred to the top class as 'the bosses', leading the researchers to suggest that there could be a latent proletarian imagery to be found in male manual workers living in integrated working-class communities. Hiller (1975a), in Australia, found this kind of model held by 46 per cent of unskilled manual workers, compared with 5 per cent of semi-skilled, and 4 per cent of skilled manual workers. (Interestingly, the model was also held by 5 per cent of white-collar workers.) Davis and Cousins (1975) question whether this model is a sociological or a historical construct and suggest that knowledge of past working-class images of society is sparse – suggesting that there is no evidence that it ever was a dominant working-class model of society, despite Lockwood's label of 'traditional'. It is not surprising, therefore, that this is *not* a dominant image among male manual workers in traditional industries in contemporary capitalist societies.

Lockwood's second type, the privatized worker, is to be found typically in newer industries with relatively high pay; pay is said to be his chief interest, and he has an instrumental attitude to politics and trade unionism (see Goldthorpe *et al.* 1969). The model of society held by this group is one in which class differences are seen chiefly in terms of money and possessions and in which the bulk of people, both manual and non-manual, are said to belong to the same class. Goldthorpe *et al.* found that 54 per cent of the manual workers in their Luton sample held this model. Other research has certainly indicated a group whose model of class includes a large central class, variously referred to as a middle class, a working class, or a lower class (see, for example, Roberts *et al.* 1977; Britten 1984). Roberts *et al.* deny that this image is prevalent as a working-class view of society. Nevertheless, they do argue that 25 per cent of their manual sample have a middle-class model of society – a diamond-shaped distribution of class membership where they placed themselves in the largest class, in the middle. These apparently bourgeois manual workers typically had strong white-collar connections, owned their own houses, and held to conventional middle-class values. (Surprisingly, Roberts *et al.* do not seem to have considered whether these values could be related to the occupations or class backgrounds of the wives of the manual workers who held this social imagery.) In contrast, Hiller (1975a) argued that a large number of both the manual and the non-manual workers in his sample used what might loosely be described as a 'money model'. However, to refer to most or all of the respondents as having a money model is to confound a number of different images with different combinations of objective and evaluative criteria used in determining class. Also, Platt (1971), in a critical evaluation of the Affluent Worker Study, argues that the authors of that study may have been in error in attributing a money model to so many of the affluent workers. She suggests that money is only one factor used in determining class placement and that indeed a stress on money as a determinant of class is not incompatible with a traditional proletarian model.

Lockwood's third ideal type was the deferential traditional worker, who was seen as having a close and paternalistic relationship with the employer and limited opportunities for forming strong attachments to other workers; the farm worker is regarded as a prototypical example. Deferential workers, according to the typification, would have a hierarchical model of society with at least four classes which would be said to differ in terms of status. Lockwood based the model on voting research carried out in England during the 1960s (e.g. Samuel 1960; Stacey 1960; Abrams 1961; Plowman 1962; Mackenzie and Silver 1964; Runciman 1966). Despite much research aimed at locating this deferential worker, however, he has proved elusive (Newby 1979; Batstone 1975; Carter 1974; Roberts *et al.* 1977; Curran 1978).

Less attention has been paid, both by theorists and in empirical research, to the images of society held by non-manual workers. Lockwood studied male clerical workers in the 1950s and argued that in terms of class, status, and power they correctly perceived themselves as 'above' manual workers. Roberts *et al.* suggest that it is the lack of empirical research that has led to the myth of a unitary middle-class imagery. They suggest that the middle class is, in fact, fragmented and that at least three distinct social images can be discerned. The most common (though still not held by a majority) sees the middle class as the largest group, occupying the middle ground in the class structure. The working class is seen as a small class consisting of scroungers, the unemployed, layabouts, and so on. (However, division within the middle class is perceived, and a 'ladder' view of mobility is held, with a strong desire to be upwardly mobile in a system that is seen as permitting such mobility.) The second group is typically comprised of the self-employed; they see the middle class as a small group between large upper and working classes. The third image is that of the white-collar proletariat, the 14 per cent of their sample who identified with the working class. Roberts *et al.* stress, further-more, that these three sets of images do not exhaust the variation in their sample. One further important group to which they point, for example, are the middle-class radicals – well-educated professionals who hold radical political views (usually of the left) and radical social ideals. Hiller (1975a) also points to the importance of divisions within the middle class and dis-tinguishes between professional/managerial workers and white-collar workers. The vast majority of the former (76.5 per cent in his study) select models that combine 'objective' determinants of class (education, income, occupation, etc.) with prestige criteria (style of life, family background, etc.). White-collar workers were more diverse in type: 5 per cent appeared to hold a power model, 18 per cent a 'snobbishness' dichotomy, 32 per cent held models based mainly on objective criteria, and 14 per cent a model grounded in a mixture of objective and prestige criteria. Only 14 per cent overall held a class prestige model such as is usually attributed to the middle class by theorists.

In terms of working-class images of society, then, different researchers have elicited rather different models but, as Moor-house (1976) argues, the respondents in all these studies have a tendency to see themselves as in the largest social class and to stress money as a key factor in class divisions. As far as middle-class images are concerned, the debate has most recently concentrated on the proletarianization of the clerical worker (Braverman 1980) – the argument being that changes in the type and conditions of work and in relative income mean that routine non-manual workers can no longer be differentiated from the manual working class. It has been argued that this is specifically true of routine white-collar workers, who perform unskilled or semi-skilled jobs, earn low wages, and have little chance of promotion (Crompton and Jones 1984). However, Davis (1979) has pointed out that whatever the objective conditions of clerical work may be in relation to manual work, social consciousness may lag behind or leap ahead of changes in material conditions. In his study of male clerical workers he found that they all thought of themselves as middle-class – that is, they placed themselves in the middle of a hierarchy rather than at either end. The terms they used most frequently to describe their class position were 'middle-class' or 'lower middle-class'. They were not class-conscious in terms of identifying with a class in opposition to other classes, but saw class rather as an expression of a person's place in the social system, an outcome of personal efforts and abilities. The social system was seen as open and just. In terms of political allegiance a majority (68 per cent) identified with the Conservative Party, while only a small minority (11 per cent) identified with the Labour Party. With respect to work, they held a unitary conception of the firm – everyone working together to achieve a common goal. Davis concluded that clerical workers had a fragmentary and confused picture of society, but one clearly differentiated from the social imagery of the working class. Hiller (1975a), however, concluded that white-collar workers had very similar imagery to that of the skilled working class, and equally fragmented, both these strata being different in this respect from semi- and unskilled workers. Abbott (1987), in an analysis of the female routine non-manual workers in the People in Society Survey, concluded that their social imagery was comparable to that found among the Davis (1979) and Roberts *et al.* (1977) samples of male routine non-manual workers.

The research discussed so far has carried an expectation that there will be a relationship between objective social class and subjective awareness of the class structure. However, Graetz (1983), analysing data collected in Australia, challenges this view. He argues that class imagery is not predictable from information about objective social class alone, but that there are clear differences based on *subjective* social class – although he also argues that there is in general a consensual view about class and social inequalities in Australia. A clear majority of his respondents depicted classes in terms of status or prestige differences such as income, possessions, where and how people live, and educational qualifications, and they ranked people along a single social scale, emphasising interests different people share. However, those who identified themselves as 'upper-class' placed more emphasis on individual ability and willingness to work and appeared to be more concerned with issues of power control, although this rarely extended beyond material interests. However, when voting behaviour was examined, it was found that a majority of people who identified themselves as middle- or upper-class voted Conservative, while a majority of those who saw themselves as working-class voted Labour (including those who had a consensual social imagery).

Thus while previous research has stressed the existence of social imagery and the links between a person's subjective understanding of the social structure and their objective location within it, care must be taken not to try to 'fit' responses to preconceived ideal types too rigidly. Indeed, while much of the research has drawn on the ideal types, most researchers have concluded that there is at best fragmentary class-awareness and that a number of respondents have too confused an image for them to be classified in the research. Also past research has established the importance of examining the links between class position, conceptions of the class structure, and class sentiment/class action, but that at the same time it has indicated that these links may not be direct or simple ones.

Women's class imagery

A criticism of the greater part of research on class images (indeed, as we have seen, of class research in general) is its tendency to ignore women. Most of the studies referred to above included only men in their samples and presumably either assume that the results are generalizable to women or that women's class images are of no theoretical significance. (Roberts *et al.* justify their failure to include women by the fact that previous research had not included them and that if women were included they would therefore not be able to compare their study with previous ones!) When women *are* included in such research they are generally categorized according to their husbands' or fathers' occupations rather than according to their own. This often leads to confusing and contradictory results. It is usually argued or implied (Mackenzie 1975) that the major determinant of class imagery is work experience, although other factors have also been seen as influential. This seems to suggest that a woman's social imagery and subsequent class action are more likely to be shaped by her own work experience and primary group membership than by her husband's occupation, though to the extent that her husband's occupation enables her to enjoy a particular lifestyle and pattern of consumption it may be one factor in shaping her imagery.

One study which did include women and categorize them according to own occupation is reported by Britten (1984), and it suggests that women's social class imagery may differ from that of men. The men in her sample who were in manual occupations tended to have a two-class model, placing themselves in the lower class, and the non-manual men a three-class model, placing themselves in the middle. The women, irrespective of class, inclined towards the latter image – a diamond-shaped structure comprised of three classes, with themselves in the middle stratum; this was particularly true of the married women in the sample – although, as we have already pointed out, there is considerable overlap in people's everyday understanding of the social structure, and only a small minority of respondents in any study report clear class images in precisely ideal-typical form.

In previous research (again mostly on male samples), one frequently used measure of class sentiment or class action has been voting behaviour (see, for example, Jackman and Jackman 1983; Graetz 1983). In line with the 'party identification' theory of voting, it is assumed that individuals vote for the party which they see as representing their class or its interests – the working-class manual worker for the Labour Party, and the middle class for the Conservative Party. As we saw in Chapter 5, this theory of voting behaviour has been challenged – in part at least because of a degree of de-alignment observable in recent years – by the 'policy preference' model. However, we argued that despite the decline in the share of votes experienced by both main parties and especially by the Labour Party in the 1970s and 1980s, none the less the majority of support for the main parties still comes from the expected classes. Also there is some evidence (Crewe 1983) that identification with Labour has not declined as much as its share of the vote did between 1979 and 1983. We shall therefore include political preference in our analysis as one aspect of the 'image of society'.

Graetz has pointed, indeed, to the importance of voting behaviour as an aid in interpreting social images, and the importance of not *assuming* that a given apparent pattern of social imagery has a necessary relationship to the way people vote, but rather using voting if necessary to discriminate between apparently identical patterns of social imagery. On the other hand, Porter (1983) found male manual workers in her research who identified strongly with the working class and were heavily involved in trade unionism and strike action but who none the less voted Conservative. (Their wives were often opposed to trade unionism but strong supporters of the Labour Party.) It is unsafe, then, to assume any particular theory of the origins of voting behaviour when interpreting such data.

The rest of this chapter will look at the social images held by the women in the People in Society Survey – the number of classes they see, their perception of the possibility and desirability of social mobility, whether they see conflict as a dominant 'fact' of society, their subjective social class, what they see as the main determinants of class, political identification – to see whether consistent and interpretable 'clusters' can be found. Interpretation will be aided by analysis in terms of objective class and educational level. In this way we hope to begin a determination, within the limitations of the data, of whether women have coherent mental maps of the social structure and whether these appear comparable to the ones previous research had identified as held by men.

We are aware, however, that the overall result of the research on men must be taken as a failure to find coherent images; very many respondents in previous studies appear to hold confounded imagery that cannot readily be 'typed'. We are also aware of the strong tendency to look for 'ideal types' and to fit the data to these, sometimes rather arbitrarily, rather than letting the data 'speak for themselves' or at least trying to use the full range of complexity of the data. Thus Platt (1971) has demonstrated how the dominant money model said in the original publications to have been found among the Affluent Worker sample is open to doubt if answers to the other questions on the questionnaire are also taken into account. Townsend (1979) has suggested that what are often claimed to be two opposed ideal types – the middle-class prestige model and the working-class power model – are in fact commonly combined both in sociological discourse and in people's everyday understanding of the social structure. We cannot hope to overcome these problems of social imagery research in our analysis, because the questions asked in this survey were based on those commonly employed in previous studies (on male samples). For this reason our respondents will to some extent have been conditioned to answer in terms that will produce the kinds of model that have been produced in the past. However, we intend to let the data speak for themselves in the sense that we shall analyse first in terms of frequency of clustered responses, before trying to fit the models that have been elicited in previous studies of men and seeing whether they can be said to apply to women.

Images in the 'People in Society' survey

We have already seen, in Chapters 4 and 5, that the majority of the women in this survey agreed on the existence of social classes in modern Britain and were prepared to place themselves in a social class. There was a strong relationship between this 'subjective' social class and objective class as determined by occupation (whether we used own occupation or the more conventional criterion of head of household's occupation). When we came to look at how they saw the social structure, the criteria they used to place people in social classes and their voting behaviour there was less evidence of a class split – in other words, there was both disagreement within classes and considerable agreement between classes. None the less, there did seem to be some evidence that subjective class was related to class imagery (as was objective class), though in no direct, one-to-one way. The rest of this chapter attempts to explore the relationship between these factors in more detail. When we looked at images of the class structure in Chapter 5 we based our analysis on three key factors: how many social classes respondents thought there were, whether they saw mobility as possible and desirable, and whether they saw conflict or consensus as characteristic of society. Only a tiny proportion of either sex in the sample (0.1 per cent – five people) appeared to have no 'image' at all, answering 'don't know' to all three of these questions.

Using the answers to these three questions and looking only at the female respondents we found eleven combinations that were chosen by more than 3 per cent of the sample. The most popular, chosen by 899 women (34 per cent), might be considered a middle-class model – several classes, social mobility possible, and no conflict between classes. A further 183 (7 per cent) thought social mobility possible and did not consider conflict prevalent but thought there were only two classes in society, and 120 (5 per cent) thought everyone in the same class but otherwise agreed. Thus on these criteria some 46 per cent of the sample held what appears to be a middle-class model of society. Conversely, only a small proportion of the sample held what might be seen as a proletarian model. The ideal-typical proletarian model – two classes, no mobility, class conflict – was held by 86 women (3 per cent of the sample). A further 113 (4 per cent) thought mobility not possible and conflict prevalent but saw several classes in Britain.

Initially the imagery of the rest of the sample appeared to be confused, at least in terms of the ideal-typical images discussed in the research literature. Thus 109 (4 per cent) thought there were two classes and that there was class conflict but thought social mobility possible. A further 253 (10 per cent) saw conflict as prevalent but thought there were several classes and mobility between them. A sizeable proportion of the women thought mobility not possible (a reflection of their own situation, perhaps) but that there was no conflict between the classes. Of these 114 (4 per cent) thought there were two classes, 87 (3 per cent) saw everyone as in the same class, and 245 (9 per cent) identified several classes. Finally, a small but significant number – 99 (4 per cent) – saw modern Britain as comprised of several classes with no conflict between them but 'did not know' if social mobility was possible. These simple models, based on whether or not class conflict is thought to be prevalent in modern Britain and whether or not social mobility is possible, accounted for about 88 per cent of the sample.

We attempted to go beyond this simple analysis to include more variables and to let the women to some extent 'speak for themselves' rather than looking for ideal types. Exploratory cluster analysis of a substantial 'pool' of variables suggested four which would distinguish reasonably stable clusters of women – subjective class, whether or not conflict was seen as prevalent, whether Britain was seen as divided into two classes or not, and what were seen as the determinants of class (objective status criteria, objective proletarian criteria, or subjective criteria, in the terms outlined in the last chapter). Sevety-seven per cent of the sample fell in one of the ten clusters illustrated in *Table 68*. The largest cluster comprised 25 per cent of the sample, and the smallest 2 per cent. Four of the clusters contained women who identified themselves as middle-class, and six of women who identified themselves as working-class.

The four middle-class models accounted for 40 per cent of the sample. The largest (25 per cent) was made up of women who saw themselves as middle-class, thought either that there were several classes in modern Britain or that everyone falls in the same class, saw no class conflict, and thought that social class was determined at least in part by objective status criteria and not at all by objective proletarian ones. We will refer to this as Model I. Model II, held by 7 per cent, was similar except that the women thought conflict prevalent. Model III was like Model I except that subjective rather than objective status criteria were identified as the determinants of class. Model IV was different, containing women who thought there were two classes, thought of themselves as middle-class, and saw social class as at least in part determined by subjective factors.

The other six clusters were working-class ones – or at least, held by women who considered themselves working-class. The largest, Model V (held by 11 per cent of the sample), saw no conflict in society, saw either several or one class in modern Britain but not two, and considered class determined at least in part by objective status criteria and not by objective proletarian ones. This can be seen as the working-class counterpart of Model I. Model VI, held by 4 per cent, was the same as Model V

Table 68 Social imagery clusters: Composition

model	number	% sample	subjective class	defining characteristics conflict?	defining characteristics no. of classes	determinants of class
I	661	25	Middle	No	Not 2	Objective Status, *not Objective Proletarian*
II	181	7	Middle	Yes	Not 2	Objective Status, *not Objective Proletarian*
III	140	5	Middle	No	Not 2	Subjective
IV	114	4	Middle	—	2	*not Objective Status*, Subjective
V	283	11	Working	No	Not 2	Objective Status, *not Objective Proletarian*
VI	117	4	Working	Yes	Not 2	Objective Status, *not Objective Proletarian*
VII	65	2	Working	No	Not 2	Subjective, *not Objective Status*
VIII	113	4	Working	—	2	Subjective, *not Objective Status*
IX	93	4	Working	No	2	*Not Subjective*
X	127	5	Working	Yes	2	*Not Subjective*

Note
For definitions of the categories used to describe determinants of class see Chapter 7.

except that class conflict was seen as prevalent – the working-class equivalent of Model II. Model VII – held by 2 per cent – was made up of women who saw society in the same way as those in Model V except that they mentioned subjective criteria as determinants of class – the working-class equivalent of Model III – and Model VIII, similarly, parallels Model IV, containing women who did see two classes in society and thought class at least in part determined by subjective criteria. The final two clusters are identical except for one major difference: Model IX women (held by 4 per cent) define themselves as working-class, see society as divided into two classes, see no class conflict, and do not mention subjective factors as determinants of class; Model X is like this except that the women do see class conflict in contemporary Britain.

Descriptive analysis of the women in each cluster did not suggest that these images were necessarily held by coherent clusters of women, however. Thus Model I was held predominantly by women who were objectively middle-class by their own job if in employment (74 per cent of the relevant base), living in households headed by a middle-class person (83 per cent), but that leaves a substantial objectively working-class residue. Over two-thirds of the women in this cluster had stayed on at school for two or more years past the minimum leaving age, and a similar proportion held educational qualifications at or higher than GCE 'A' level. Over three-quarters (82 per cent) thought social mobility possible and desirable, and 52 per cent voted Conservative (with a further 22 per cent supporting the Alliance). This is clearly, then, a middle-class model, held in general by relatively successful women.

Model III was like Model I except that the women who held it favoured subjective over objective status criteria as determinants of class. These women were similar to those who held Model I in terms of own objective and household class, but were less likely to have stayed on at school – 50 per cent left at the minimum age – and 43 per cent held educational qualifications lower than 'A' level or none at all. A much smaller proportion thought mobility possible (64 per cent), and support for the Conservative Party and the Alliance were slightly lower at 49 per cent and 16 per cent, respectively.

Model II differed from Models I and III in that the women

who held it saw class conflict in contemporary Britain. The employed women in this group were predominantly in non-manual jobs (79 per cent), as were 75 per cent of their heads of household. In educational terms these women fell between the other two clusters, just over half having stayed on at school for 2+ years and just under half having qualifications at 'A' level or better. Over three-quarters thought social mobility possible and desirable, but support for the Labour Party was higher and for the Conservatives and the Alliance lower than in the other two clusters. Moreover, there were curious discontinuities by marital and employment status. While 39 per cent voted Labour overall, 29 per cent Conservative, and 28 per cent Liberal or SDP, the single women and the full-time housewives supported Labour more heavily than the employed married women (56 per cent and 46 per cent respectively, compared with 36 per cent). Conversely, only 8 per cent of the single women supported the Conservative Party, but 25 per cent of the full-time housewives and 37 per cent of the employed married women. In terms of class action, therefore, this model does not represent a cohesive group of women.

The women holding Model IV were clearly even less cohesive. These women identified themselves as middle-class; see two classes in society, and nominate subjective criteria as important in determining class. They were split on whether social mobility was possible (two-thirds said that it was) and on whether conflict exists in Britain (80 per cent said it does). In terms of occupational class, the employed members of this cluster came from across the range: the single women came mainly from routine non-manual occupations (65 per cent), with 15 per cent in professional or managerial employment and 18 per cent in manual jobs; the married women were mostly in routine non-manual work (40 per cent) or semi- or unskilled work (38 per cent). More voted for the Conservatives (34 per cent) than for Labour (24 per cent) or the Alliance (25 per cent). In terms of education the majority had some qualification, and they were as likely to have stayed on beyond the minimum age as to have left. Clearly this cluster of women do not in any real terms share an imagery.

The other six clusters were working-class ones in terms of subjective class identification, although not all of the women in them held manual jobs or lived in households with a working-class

Table 69 Social imagery clusters: Descriptive analysis

model	head of household's class		father's class		own class[1]		years of post-compulsory education %			educational qualifications			party preference		
	Mid.	Wor.	Mid.	Wor.	Mid.	Wor.	0	1	2+	None	<A[2]	A+[3]	Lab.	Con.	All.
I	84	16	67	33	84	16	23	12	65	9	16	75	10	52	22
II	71	29	69	31	77	23	33	16	51	16	22	62	39	29	16
III	77	23	53	47	82	18	50	12	38	21	21	58	17	49	16
IV	36	64	40	60	57	43	49	14	37	35	22	43	24	34	25
V	32	68	34	66	48	52	71	9	20	47	27	26	38	23	16
VI	15	85	20	80	33	67	82	7	11	62	25	13	66	13	8
VII	37	63	26	74	39	61	64	16	20	28	38	34	35	25	29
VIII	18	82	22	78	17	83	84	5	11	51	27	22	48	12	12
IX	22	78	19	81	39	61	73	12	15	47	33	20	48	13	12
X	14	86	17	83	22	78	85	5	10	63	21	16	77	7	5

1 For employed women only.
2 Less than GCE 'A' level.
3 'A' level or higher.

head. Model X comes nearest to representing a proletarian class imagery – two classes, conflict and class determined at least in part by 'objective proletarian' criteria. However, 59 per cent held that social mobility was possible, and about a fifth were in non-manual occupations. On the other hand, the majority left school at the minimum legal age (85 per cent), 63 per cent had no educational qualifications, and a further 21 per cent had no qualification above 'O' level. The vast majority supported the Labour Party – 77 per cent, with only 7 per cent voting Conservative and 5 per cent Alliance.

The only other working-class cluster in which the women perceived social conflict was the one holding Model VI. These differed from the Model X cluster in that they saw class as determined by subjective criteria, although some of them mentioned objective proletarian criteria as well; they also thought there were several classes in Britain today. The women in this group were similar to those holding Model X in that they left school at the first opportunity (82 per cent), and had no qualifications (62 per cent) or few (20 per cent). The majority of those who were employed had manual jobs, but 22 per cent were in professional or managerial positions and 16 per cent in routine non-manual ones. However, the vast majority (73 per cent) lived in households with a manual head. A majority (66 per cent) voted Labour; 13 per cent supported the Conservatives and 8 per cent the Alliance. This too could be seen as a fairly conventionally working-class group and might be combined with Model X.

Models V and VII were held by women who see themselves as working-class but do not think there is class conflict in modern Britain; they differed in what they see as determinants of class – Model V prefers objective status criteria and Model VII subjective ones. The two groups are similar in their composition: about 60 per cent of the employed women were in manual jobs, and about 60 per cent lived in households with a manual head. Just over a third supported the Labour party (38 per cent for Model V and 35 per cent for Model VII), while around a quarter supported the Conservatives (23 per cent and 25 per cent); however, 29 per cent of the Model V women voted Alliance, but only 14 per cent of the Model VII women. Those in the Model VII cluster are slightly less likely to have stayed on at school (71 per cent left at the minimum age, compared with 64 per cent) or to have educational qualifications (47 per cent were unqualified, compared with 28 per cent). There seems some possibility that a recognizably working-class imagery underlies these two clusters, but there is considerable confusion within them.

Cluster IX is made up of subjectively working-class women who see only two classes (not in conflict) and consider class determined by objective factors. A bare majority (58 per cent) of those in employment were in manual jobs, but 72 per cent lived in households with a manual head. The majority (73 per cent) left school at the minimum age, and over 80 per cent had low educational qualifications or none at all. However, there is no clear pattern to their voting behaviour or their perception of social mobility: 45 per cent thought mobility possible and 48 per cent voted Labour, with 32 per cent supporting the Conservatives, and 12 per cent the Alliance. Again there may be a cohesive imagery underlying this group but on the surface the cohesion is far from evident.

The final cluster is the women holding Model VIII, who defined themselves as working-class, thought there were two classes in society, and saw class as defined at least partly by subjective criteria. A majority of those in employment (80 per cent) had working-class jobs, and a similar proportion lived in households with a manual head. The majority (84 per cent) left school at the earliest opportunity, and 79 per cent had 'O' levels or less. Just over half (54 per cent) saw mobility as possible, and about two-thirds (68 per cent) did not see conflict between the classes. In terms of voting the most support went to Labour (48 per cent), but 21 per cent supported the Conservatives and 12 per cent the Alliance. While this cluster is obviously working-class in terms of the women's occupations, it has no obvious cohesive imagery.

What this analysis clearly tells us is that while there may appear to be considerable agreement about the nature of the class structure at the level of single variables, the overall social imagery of the women in this sample is fragmented and appears confused. In particular, we note that class action, as measured by party preference, does not appear to correlate closely with other aspects of class imagery. Furthermore, while objective criteria such as occupation and education do show some correlation with social imagery, a substantial minority of the women appear to hold social images which would be more typical of women who differ from them significantly on these objective criteria.

Nevertheless there appears to be evidence that middle-class social images can be distinguished from working-class ones, though with considerable overlap. The major differences tend to be based on occupation, education, voting behaviour, and subjective social class, as would be expected. Thus the major factors distinguishing the middle class from the working class are that the former define themselves as middle-class, generally have a non-manual occupation, have stayed on at school beyond the minimum age, have qualifications at 'A' level or higher, and vote for the Conservative Party or the Alliance. Conversely, the latter define themselves as working-class, left school at the earliest opportunity and/or with few or no qualifications, have manual or routine non-manual jobs, and support the Labour Party. Many of the respondents, whether middle- or working-class, combine elements of prestige, proletarian, and money models. This is perhaps not surprising given that social science and common sense discourse define class, class conflict, and social mobility in different ways. (Consider, for example, the differences between Weberian and Marxist definitions of class, class conflict, and mobility, let alone the ways in which we use the terms in our everyday lives.) What people see as the determinants of class, whether they think the classes are in conflict, and whether they think social mobility possible are unlikely to be stable and coherent 'traits', and the answers given may well depend on what respondents thought the questioner meant. Class is a confusing and a confounded concept, and it seems to us not surprising that social images do not appear coherent and class-specific but are confused and fragmented compared with the social science concepts.

Despite the reservations expressed above and the results outlined in the last section, we decided to see if we could 'find' in our sample the ideal-typical class images found in previous malestream research. Given that the questions asked were based on this previous research, it would after all be surprising if we did not find a proportion of our sample holding these images. On the basis of previous research we decided to look for what might be seen as ideal-typical middle-class and working-class models, and we started with subjective determining/categorizing factors – subjective class, voting behaviour, perception of the determinants of class, and images of the class structure.

The classical 'middle-class' image was not difficult to find. Forty per cent of the sample (1,019 women) saw society as *not* made up of two classes but as one single class or several, believed mobility to be possible and desirable, and saw society as characterized by harmony rather than conflict; of these, 710 (28 per cent of the sample) considered themselves to be middle-class. Only 345 (14 per cent of the sample) expressed a preference for the Conservative Party, but the figure rises to 499 (20 per cent) if Alliance voters are included. Excluding those who used 'objective proletarian' characteristics as determinants of class did not bring the figures down much – 429 (17 per cent) remain. Thus 17 per cent of the sample could be described as classically middle-class. Demographic characteristics confirm the description: the women are overwhelmingly in households with a middle-class head, come from middle-class families (though some small degree of intergenerational social mobility may be noted), and those in employment were overwhelmingly in middle-class jobs.

A further 6 per cent of the sample fit this description except that they identify with the working- rather than the middle-class. Two-thirds are an exact match except on subjective class; the remaining third have the additional difference of a political preference for Labour. The former group are less clearly middle-class in demographic terms: they are about as likely to have a working-class as a middle-class head of household, and rather more likely to have had a working-class father, but of those in employment a large majority (79 per cent) had middle-class jobs. The Labour voters were similar except that they were as likely to have a working-class as a middle-class job if in employment.

The classic working-class ideal types of the research literature, however, were far more difficult to find. One could identify a 'proletarian' group – seeing two classes in society (or several, as acknowledging the existence of a middle class is not incompatible with proletarian imagery), doubting the possibility of mobility, seeing society as characterized by conflict, voting Labour, and considering class determined at least in part by 'objective proletarian' considerations. The group is very small in size, however – only 2 per cent of the sample – and even deleting the limitation on 'determinants of class' increases it only to 3 per cent. The 'deferential worker' of the literature was even more elusive, as most researchers subsequent to Lock-wood have found. We found 245 people (10 per cent of the sample) who saw several classes, little mobility, and a society characterized by harmony rather than conflict, but only 108 who saw themselves as working-class, and only 15 (0.6 per cent of the sample) who voted Conservative. (Interestingly, 54 – 2 per cent – voted Labour.) Finally, we looked for a working-class money model. We found that this model, said to be so prevalent among affluent working-class males, was held by only 4 per cent of our sample, and of these only half supported the Labour Party.

Conclusions

We can conclude, then, that women do recognize the existence of social classes, are prepared to place themselves in a social class, and have a social imagery that does not seem to be totally determined by the occupational class of their head of house-hold. Furthermore, despite the fact that the questionnaire was developed on the basis of previous research into class imagery, only a small proportion of the *working-class* women in this sample held the ideal-typical social images found in that research. As in research on male samples, the images of the women were fragmentary and appeared less coherent the more criteria we included. Nevertheless, there did appear to be distinct middle-class and working-class images, the former held by a substantial minority of the sample, the latter by only a small minority. It would seem to us that the differences between the social imagery found in this survey and what has been found in previous research on males are not surprising given the different experiences of men and women in our society. Women are less likely than men, especially if in a non-manual occupation, to experience intragenerational mobility. Women are less likely to work in industries with considerable levels of industrial conflict, and working-class women are less likely to be integrally involved in trade union activity. We would suggest that women's experiences at work shape their social imagery at least in part, and, as one of us (Abbott 1987) has previously noted, this is equally true of women in routine non-manual jobs. It is evident that a married woman's class identification and imagery is shaped by the consumption class of the household (and thus, indirectly in part by her partner's occupational class). However, we suspect this is probably true for men also, and some evidence for this has been indicated in previous research on men (e.g. Goldthorpe *et al*. 1969), although it has largely been ignored.

We would conclude that the images held by the women in this sample suggested that only a small proportion are class-conscious in the sense of seeing themselves as in a class that is distinct from and has different interests from other classes. More middle-class than working-class women seem to be conscious of class in this sense, but still only a minority. While we are not convinced that previous research on men has conclusively demonstrated the existence of class consciousness among men, it would certainly seem to suggest more class consciousness among working-class men than we have found among working-class women. This is an important finding; to the extent to which women influence men in the private sphere this may help to account for the lack of class militancy among working-class males. Thus it is probably not just the existence of cross-class marriages that reduces the growth of full class consciousness, but also the different social images held by men and women – women's social images being, we suggest, a reflection of their experiences as women, as wives and daughters, and as women located in particular industries and generally excluded from participation in the trade unions. Thus when we examine social imagery from the woman's perspective it is vital to take account of subjective factors – how women see themselves. Indeed we would argue, as Graetz does, that this is equally true for men – social class imagery must incorporate subjective factors such as class identification, views on the determinants/correlates of class, and class action variables such as voting behaviour, trade union membership, and membership of other political groups (including women's groups) as well as 'objective' factors such as market class and consumption class. It is only thus that we will begin to see if class images have an affinity for classes and are held by distinct social groups. Failure to incorporate these factors and to recognize that objective class cannot be determined by occupation alone may be a central explanation of the fragmentary, confused imagery generally found and its lack of 'fit' with political action.

7 Summary and discussion

The results of the survey

This book has drawn on an analysis of data, collected between 1980 and 1984, from the Open University People in Society Survey, a national survey carried out by students on two of the Open University's research methods courses, to examine and illustrate the importance of including women in discussions of social class. The survey collected over 5,000 cases during the period, of whom some 2,500 were women, and it is unique among large-scale British surveys (with the exception of the one reported by Martin and Roberts 1984) in that it sampled women in their own right rather than just taking a sample of the wives of male respondents and that it recorded information on women's own occupation, income, etc. as well as that of their husband or other head of household. The interviewers were only partly trained, but as mature students (and often already researchers, lecturers, social workers, teachers, nurses, or others concerned in the 'people trades') their initial qualification was often far higher than would normally be expected in a national survey using an interview force which is not part of the research team. The major fault of the survey is that it used quota sampling – necessarily, given the requirement that it be carried out by widely dispersed students in a limited amount of time – and there are consequent biases in the sample as compared with Census data (see Chapter 2). However, we have argued that these seldom impede interpretation of the data, and where comparable results are available from the 'research literature' on women and class they generally agree very closely with the survey's findings.

The first and most obvious thing to note is that women's relationship to the labour market and the world of work is very different from that of men. The distribution of jobs for women has changed dramatically within living memory, with a vast increase in routine non-manual work since the Second World War; most of the positions thus created have gone to women. Women are also concentrated in other jobs – service roles, unskilled or semi-skilled manual labour (it has indeed been argued that one of the defining characteristics of the label 'skilled' when applied to a job is that it shall be carried out pre-dominantly by men, as positions which seem to require similar levels of education and training in industries where women predominate are generally denied this label). Women are also rarer in the professional and managerial classes than men. Men, by comparison, are concentrated in the professional and managerial classes and in skilled manual work, and are partic-ularly rare among routine non-manual workers. This 'labour market segmentation' and the consequent asymmetry of class distributions for men and women in the labour market are not specific to the British Isles: they appear to be typical of the Western industrial world, from Finland to the USA. Women's intergenerational mobility is therefore confused by the predo-minance of C1 occupations; women from A or B backgrounds appear to be downwardly mobile, and women from C2 backgrounds downwardly mobile into D or upwardly mobile into C1, in ways which are very much a product of market structure – of the abundance of C1 jobs for women and the relative dearth of C2 jobs and jobs at a professional or manager-ial level. Over and above this we find some limited evidence for class closure: daughters of men in the highest occupational category are more likely themselves to be in higher-level occupations, though the effect is not as marked as in comparable analyses of male intergenerational mobility, and daughters of fathers in Class D are themselves more likely to be in class D jobs. We found a small amount of longer-range mobility, from C2 or D fathers to daughters in Class B, but the amount was very small. As in analyses of male careers, we found that edu-cation – staying on at school and/or achieving educational qualifications – was markedly related to current occupational level. The *intra*generational position appears to be different for women and men, however. Men's ultimate job level is determined in part by initial qualifications but also in part by their rising in level during their work lives, while the level of women's early jobs is often the highest that they will achieve during their working lives; indeed, women who return to paid employment after a period of child care are likely to be downwardly mobile, particularly if they return to part-time rather than full-time employment. 'Countermobility' is also, therefore, a less common phenomenon among women than among men; to enter the labour market at a lower level than that of one's father but to rise to the same level is a fairly common occurrence among men, but less common among women. Many of these findings from the survey or from the literature are not solely related to the fact that women acquire domestic and child-related duties on marriage and are therefore less committed to 'careers'. Analysis of career patterns and job levels of single women suggests that they experience more upward mobility than their married sisters, but still less than men; being of the female gender is in itself a handicap in the labour market.

We have argued that our analysis of female social mobility has several important consequences for class theory – that class theory which is based on male data alone is inadequate. For example, the Oxford Mobility Study, one of the major mobility studies of recent years, set out among other things to test concepts of social closure and the existence of 'buffer zones' – in other words, the relative lack of possibilities for mobility, and the existence of 'areas' within the class hierarchy which were achievable by those from low origins and therefore gave the impression of an open and meritocratic society but in fact acted as barriers to further mobility. Another thesis they tested was the view that intragenerational mobility is no longer of any significance, job level being determined in large part by initial qualification. On the basis of their data they were strongly inclined to reject all three theses. The People in Society data and the rest of the research literature on women, however, would suggest that all three are at least partly true for women: there is a strong association between father's and daughter's job-level, particularly at the extremes of the distribution – but women are nevertheless effectively kept out of high status occupations (gender closure); the C1 job level (routine non-manual work) is attainable by women from manual working-class backgrounds but appears to be largely the highest level thus attainable, and women's job levels are very much influenced by the amount of their schooling and the level of their educational qualifications. If Goldthorpe *et al.* are right about men, therefore, it would appear that modern Britain is to some extent two societies, partitioned by gender, and that the female one is very much less open and permeable than the male one.

We also noted in Chapter 3 that studies of intergenerational mobility give a false impression even of male mobility unless women are included in them, because of the changes that have occurred in the labour market over time. It is a commonplace of mobility studies that a part of male mobility is a product of structural changes rather than any 'openness' of British society: as manual work declines and non-manual posts become more numerous, so necessarily there is a certain amount of upward mobility on average between fathers' and sons' occupations. It is normal to apply some kind of correction, for differences in the marginal totals, to eliminate this effect and leave behind the amount of 'true' mobility. Women's participation in the labour force adds to these structural effects, however, and greatly complicates the correction factors necessary to eliminate them. In *Table 70*, for instance, the first three columns represent a conventional 'correction for structural change' for the period 1921–71: the third column gives the ratio of change in male jobs over the period, and any group which showed a change significantly greater or less than this ratio would be counted as exhibiting mobility over and above the structural changes which had occurred in the labour market over the period. Columns *d–f*, however, give similar figures for *women* in the labour market, and columns *g–i* sum the two to give overall labour-market changes. Column *i*, therefore, gives the 'true' correction factor, the changes in the overall proportion of jobs available in each category, and it is *this* which should be used to measure the non-structural mobility of subgroups within the working population. The difference between column *c* and column *i* is the second structural factor, seldom taken into account, of gender changes within the distribution of occupations, and in some categories its effect is considerable (see column *j*, which gives the ratio of male to female increases in proportion of jobs available over the period). Male jobs have increased dramatically more than female ones in the 'professional' categories, and decreased far less in the skilled manual category, and similar but less marked trends may be seen for 'administrators and

Table 70 Male, female, and total job mobility, 1921–1971

socio-economic group	males 1921 (a) %	males 1971 (b) %	ratio b/a (c)	females 1921 (d) %	females 1971 (e) %	ratio e/d (f)	total 1921 (g) %	total 1971 (h) %	ratio h/g (i)	ratio f/c (j)
Self-employed and higher-grade salaried professional workers	1.6	6.1	3.8	0.9	1.4	1.6	1.4	4.4	3.1	0.4
Employers and proprietors	7.7	5.2	0.7	4.7	2.9	0.6	6.8	4.4	0.6	0.9
Administrators and managers	4.3	9.9	2.3	2.1	3.3	1.6	3.7	7.5	2.1	0.7
Lower-grade salaried professionals and technicians	1.8	5.5	3.1	6.3	10.8	1.7	3.1	7.4	2.4	0.5
Inspectors, supervisors, and foremen (of manual workers)	1.9	4.5	2.4	0.3	1.2	4.0	1.4	3.3	2.3	1.7
Clerical workers	5.1	6.1	1.2	9.8	28.0	2.9	6.5	14.0	2.2	2.4
Sales personnel and shop assistants	4.1	3.9	1.0	7.5	9.4	1.3	5.1	5.9	1.2	1.3
Skilled manual workers	32.3	29.4	0.9	20.3	9.3	0.5	28.8	22.2	0.8	0.5
Semi-skilled manual workers	24.5	21.2	0.9	40.0	27.3	0.7	29.1	23.4	0.8	0.8
Unskilled manual workers	16.7	8.2	0.5	8.1	6.4	0.8	14.2	7.6	0.5	1.6

Reprinted from Halsey, A.H. (1978) *Change in British Society*, Table 2.1, Oxford University Press.
Note
All figures rounded to one decimal place.

managers' and semi-skilled workers. On the other hand, women's jobs have increased far more than men's in the categories of clerical workers, unskilled workers, shop personnel and 'inspectors, supervisors and foremen'. In other words, with the exception of the last-named category women have migrated to the bottom of the non-manual group and to the bottom of the manual group as well, making space for men at the top end of each category. Thus men's apparent upward mobility is in part a structural consequence of a zero-sum game, being balanced by net downward mobility for women.

Table 71, showing the more recent and familiar period from 1961 to 1981, shows again how necessary it is to include women in any analysis of changes in the labour market. Looking first at column *i*, the ratio of the 1981 proportion of total available jobs in a given category to the 1961 figures, we can see that 'higher-class' jobs have risen consistently as a proportion of the total available jobs, that junior non-manual and personal service jobs (i.e. clerks, typists, shop assistants, etc.) have remained about constant, and that all categories of manual labour (including farming) have declined (with the exception of self-employed craftsmen and jobbing workers). The overall trend masks considerable variation between the genders, however. 'Upper class' jobs have increased as a proportion of the total for both sexes (though, of course, there are still far fewer women than men in them, as there were in 1961). The decline in skilled and semi-skilled work is far more marked for women than for men, however, while the decline in agricultural labour is *less* marked for women, and the decline in unskilled work is more or less confined to the men. On the other hand, the increase in self-employed 'own account' work is also confined to men and presumably represents small-scale endeavours set up out of redundancy money and the like. In relative terms (column *j*) women have done better than men in the top professions and in managerial employment (while still being under-represented there), in junior non-manual work, in agricultural labour, in the armed forces, and as unskilled labourers or their supervisors. Men have done better than women as employed professionals, as 'intermediate' non-manual workers, as personal service workers, and as skilled or semi-skilled labour. A very familiar process is clearly illustrated – the de-skilling of jobs and the

Table 71 Changes in the labour market, 1961–1981

socio-economic group	males			females			total			
	1961 (a) %	1981 (b) %	ratio b/a (c)	1961 (d) %	1981 (e) %	ratio e/d (f)	1961 (g) %	1981 (h) %	ratio h/g (i)	ratio f/c (j)
Employers and managers										
large establishments	3.7	5.6	1.5	1.2	2.1	1.7	2.9	4.3	1.5	1.1
small establishments	6.0	9.4	1.5	3.0	4.7	1.6	5.1	7.6	1.5	1.0
Professional workers										
self-employed	0.8	1.0	1.2	0.1	0.1	1.8	0.6	0.7	1.1	1.5
employees	2.9	4.7	1.6	0.8	0.9	1.2	2.2	3.2	1.5	0.8
Other non-manual										
intermediate	3.9	7.6	1.9	9.7	14.9	1.5	5.8	10.4	1.8	0.8
junior	12.8	9.9	0.8	36.3	39.1	1.1	20.3	21.2	1.0	1.4
personal service	0.9	1.2	1.3	12.3	12.5	1.0	4.5	5.6	1.2	0.8
Manual workers										
foremen/supervisors	3.3	3.7	1.1	0.6	0.7	1.2	2.5	2.5	1.0	1.1
skilled	31.3	27.0	0.9	8.7	4.1	0.5	24.2	18.1	0.8	0.5
semi-skilled	15.1	14.0	0.9	16.2	10.9	0.7	15.5	12.8	0.8	0.7
unskilled	8.8	5.9	0.7	7.0	6.9	1.0	8.2	6.3	0.8	1.5
own account	3.7	5.8	1.6	2.7	2.0	0.7	3.4	4.3	1.3	0.5
Farming										
employers/managers	1.0	0.7	0.7	0.2	0.1	0.8	0.8	0.5	0.6	1.2
own account	1.1	0.7	0.6	0.2	0.1	0.6	0.8	0.5	0.6	1.0
labourers	2.4	1.2	0.5	0.7	0.6	0.8	1.9	1.0	0.5	1.5
Armed Forces	2.0	1.6	0.8	0.2	0.2	1.2	1.4	1.1	0.8	1.4

Sources: GRO 1966: Table 19; OPCS 1984: Table 17.

Note

The figures are for England and Wales and exclude cases classified as 'indefinite' in the 1961 Census or 'inadequately described and not stated occupations' in the 1981 Census. All figures are rounded to one decimal place.

importation of women at the bottom which so often occurs as a restructuring of the labour market during recession, decreasing the number of jobs available for men (because women are cheaper – they can be paid at unskilled rates, and many of these 'new' jobs are part-time ones). The average job level of those men who remain in employment is thereby improved, because the redundancies for men occur at the bottom of the hierarchies.

Another area of theory at which we have looked is the question of bounded classes versus one continuous hierarchy, a major point of difference between class theorists in Europe and the United States: can we talk of a 'middle' and a 'working' class as in any sense relatively closed and relatively homogeneous entities, or is it more fruitful to consider class as a continuous prestige scale without internal barriers? Our results for women would tend on the whole to support the European rather than and American position on this question. In terms of mobility, the manual/non-manual divide acts as something of a barrier; it is possible to cross it into C1, the lowest 'middle-class' category, but rare to go beyond this, and those from AB backgrounds tend on the whole to non-manual jobs while those from C2 or D backgrounds tend on the whole to manual ones. (The same partial divide is evident in statistics on class of husband as well.) Subjective self-assignment to middle or working class appears to be a task with some meaning for the women in the sample – they have little difficulty in doing it, and they do see differences between the two classes, though they may blur the boundaries a trifle. On the whole the class to which a woman assigns herself is well predicted by class of own occupation, class of husband's occupation, or class of father, with classes AB strongly associated with the middle class and classes C2D strongly associated with the working class. Class C1 appears to be a more ambiguous location, but it is associated with middle-class status by a majority of respondents, and dichotomizing between C1 and C2, at the traditional manual/non-manual border, gives the best prediction of subjective class assignment. There is little evidence here, therefore, for any supposed proletarianization of routine non-manual work, nor of unbroken continuity in the ranking of social standing.

We also examined the concept of marital mobility in chapter 3 and found it not as illuminating as has often been thought. It is true that women's class as measured by the difference between their husband's class and their father's is on the whole raised by marriage, but this 'marital mobility' is about the same in extent as male intergenerational occupational mobility, a result which echoes earlier studies in this country and the United States. This means that true marital mobility is something of an illusion, for this degree of male intergenerational mobility is largely explained by the changes in the distribution of occupations between the classes from the last generation to the present one. (It has been argued, however, that females from Class A are less likely to marry, as are males from class D, which suggests some small degree of mate selection amounting to a net social mobility by marriage.) We also noted, though on the basis of a very small sub-set of the survey respondents, that where we have information on married women's employment when they are of an age such that family formation has probably not yet disrupted their work patterns and thus the job recorded is likely to be of the same level as the one they had before marriage (if not indeed the same job), mobility measured with this job as base is about as likely to be down as up. Marriage does not appear to be a more important vehicle for female intergenerational mobility than own occupation, but if anything a less important one.

Looking at correlates of self-assigned class (middle- or working) we found that own occupation was a better predictor of subjective class for single women than was head of household's class, and indeed the latter added nothing of significance to the prediction once the former was included. For married working women, husband's occupation was the best single predictor, but own occupation was not much worse, added something independently to the prediction when the two were combined, and was in any case highly correlated with husband's class. Eliminating this correlation by looking separately at 'upward' and 'downward' cross-class marriages, we found that the same pattern held for those whose occupational class was lower than that of their husband, but where the woman's occupational class was higher than her husband's his class was a poor predictor of her subjective class, and own occupation an even poorer predictor. Husband's class also predicted the subjective class of non-employed married women, but surprisingly accounted for less of the variance than with married employed women. Among other factors which made a significant contribution over and above husband's or head of household's class were class of father, extent of post-compulsory schooling, level of educational qualification, and sometimes own or husband's income. Among single women, whether or not coded as head of household, own occupation was by far the best predictive variable, though father's class and educational qualifications added something to the prediction. The best predictive function for employed married women included (in order of entry) class of husband, years of post-compulsory education, husband's income, own occupational class, father's class, and educational qualifications. Omitting one or both of the 'husband' variables makes a significant but small change to the amount of variance explained. For non-employed married women husband's class is an important predictor, but we can explain more of the variance by father's class added to the two educational variables than by husband's class alone. The overall conclusion has to be that for married women their husband's class is an important predictor of subjective class assignment (though for those whose occupational class is higher than their husbands' it is not a very good predictor), and that own occupation is not by itself a successful predictor of subjective class. The reverse conclusion holds for single women and head of household's class, however. Moreover, while own occupation is not a good predictor for employed married women, educational variables (and perhaps father's class) *are* good predictors for all groups of women. This points the way, perhaps, towards an assignment of class to full-time housewives on some other basis than the occupational class of their husbands, and one more closely related to their own characteristics.

The only variable in the survey even vaguely approximating to a measure of *class action* was preference for political party (not just which party they last voted for, but which they generally voted for or support). As in other studies we found class not perfectly aligned with party preference, but on the whole the Conservatives still had their 'power-base' among those who saw themselves as middle-class and the Labour Party among the self-assigned working class. No combination of the variables in the survey was particularly successful at predicting support for either Conservatives or Labour – little of the variance was explained – but in so far as prediction was possible at all, subjective class tended to be the most important predictor, with educational level, own occupational class, and father's class also making some contribution. Husband's class was seldom an effective predictor, but this does not necessarily mean that husbands had no effect on party preference, as their party preference may also have followed class divisions only imperfectly.

Finally, attitude questions in the survey allowed us to look superficially at the women's views of society and images of social class – what kind of a social world they think they inhabit, and what part class plays in that picture. Social class would appear to be a meaningful and often a salient concept for the respondents: about a third mentioned 'class' spontaneously when asked about 'groups in society', and most admitted the existence of classes when asked the question direct and were prepared to place themselves in one. For the majority, the labels 'middle class' and 'working class' were sufficient description, and virtually all were able to place themselves in one or the other of those categories. However, we do not on the whole find a division in images of society along class lines such as have sometimes been reported from research on males. There are some people who see society as divided into two antagonistic classes and/or as not open to social mobility and/or as conflict-ridden, and those who tend to determine class on the basis of what might be called 'proletarian' criteria – wealth, power – and they do tend to be found among those who see themselves as working-class and would be seen as working-class on 'objective' criteria. They are very much a minority, however. The dominant picture of society, across the classes, appears to be one of harmony and mobility, in so far as we can tell from these variables. Looking at the variables in combination, we were able to identify a 'middle-class imagery' similar to what has been found in previous research on men, held by a substantial minority of the sample, but no corresponding 'proletarian imagery', whether or not in line with previous findings, was held by more than a tiny fraction. On the whole it would appear that working-class women are less coherent and class-oriented in their social imagery than working-class men, a point of some theoretical importance (see end of Chapter 6).

Thus in summary we feel this book has demonstrated that the study of women's class identification and class sentiment can make an important and a necessary contribution to class theory. We have shown that women have to be included in mobility studies in order to make full sense of the mobility of men, and that the study of female mobility can cast considerable light on the extent to which society is open to movement rather than bound by class divisions – and indeed that its apparent though limited openness for men in terms of upward mobility is bought at the price of a fair degree of closure for women. Mobility rates may be similar for men and women, but men are much more likely to be upwardly mobile, while women are downwardly mobile to a much greater extent, with more limited upward mobility.

We have shown that women do have a subjective class identification and that this is no better predicted from husband's or head of household's class than from own occupation and/or personal and 'pre-marital' attributes such as class of origin and educational level. (Predicting voting preference, our only measure of class *action*, we found that own occupation and/or background variables were, if anything, a *better* predictor than class of husband, and that self-assigned class was by far the best of a range of poor predictors.) Women's overall views of society as conflictual or harmonious and divided or homogeneous, again, were no better predicted by husband's or head of household's class than by the women's own attributes, and the same is true of their overall social imagery. The position that married women derive their class sentiments from their husbands and that single women derive them from their fathers or from whomsoever else they happen to be living with is therefore not sustainable.

What we have not shown is that women are systematically different from men in the way they view the social world and place themselves within it – that in this sense women 'form a class for themselves'. On the contrary, our results for women appear to parallel the research on men reasonably closely; they may perhaps be rather less likely than men to see society as conflictual and divided against itself, even if they are closely bound into a proletarian life position, but the differences are less large, the evidence difficult to interpret clearly, and the evidence for proletarian views among men not by any means beyond doubt. It is not surprising, however, that a questionnaire designed to elicit information on social class as previously theorized by men and for men, based in large part on previous 'malestream' research, should elicit class categories and not gender-based ones; this, after all, is its purpose. Inevitably what is found is a product in large part of the instrument through which the data were collected. The final section of the book, therefore, acts as a 'reflexive account', reviewing the survey instruments in general and the People in Society questionnaire in particular and attempting to establish the direction that future research on women's class would have to take in order to produce real advances in our understanding.

Researching women's social class

The People in Society questionnaire, applied to the question of how women see the social world, has revealed class-related rather than gender-related categories, but this must not be taken as a result of the research; rather, it is an inevitable consequence of the questionnaire's design. The questionnaire was designed to elicit class-related categories, and in its piloting and early use only those questions were retained which seemed likely to divide the population in class terms (see Henry 1981). This, after all, was its original purpose: to provide a steady stream of data on class divisions which could be analysed for student projects. Gender issues were not as salient in the sociological or psychological journals in the middle and late 1970s, when the questionnaire was designed, as they have become since. More-over, the class categories which the questionnaire is designed to tap reflect a particularly male view of the nature of class, which is in turn inevitable given the time when, and the purpose for which the questionnaire was designed. The items were culled from the literature on class, to provide possible answers to questions which were then being asked and answered by class theorists, and the questions concerned the social class of *men* because the research was all about men (and mostly working-class men). What little research there was on women by this date used these same categories; no attempt had been made to look for social categories characteristic of *women* and expressive of *women's* work and home experience; indeed, it remains to some extent true that in this as in so many other areas of sociological research women appear to be invisible to research scrutiny. Particular questions in the People in Society questionnaire clearly indicate the 'masculinity' of what is being asked. The question on the prevalence of conflict, for example, offers a choice between firms being harmonious and industry being divided into bosses and workers; there is no reflection in this of small personal service firms such as hairdressing establishments, or of one-person personal service jobs such as domestic cleaning, or of the possibility of a *three*-tier hierarchy such as might be experienced by clerical workers in industrial concerns, or of jobs where the distinction is less clear but the underlying division possibly just as deep, such as in nursing or primary school teaching or government clerical work. These are women's jobs, typically, and the categories are drawn from research into *men's* class. The very term 'worker' suggests factory labour, while the largest category of female labour is routine *non*-manual work. Sometimes, indeed, the gender bias in the questions is even more painfully explicit; one of the 'mobility' attitude items starts off 'If a man . . .'!

Class sentiments, moreover, are not a matter of personal discovery, but in the last resort of shared 'cultural' knowledge. Thus while the questions purport to tap feeling or belief, they may instead be taken by respondents as asking about knowledge, for in a sense some of them have 'right answers'. In the questions on subjective class, for instance, some people may answer 'Yes, I believe myself to be working-class', but one can equally imagine answers such as 'I suppose we are working-class – my husband's a bricklayer', or 'I suppose you'd call us working-class, as my husband's a bricklayer.' More complex variants are possible: 'I think of myself as middle-class, really, but my husband's a bricklayer, so I suppose you'd better put us down as working-class', or even 'Well, I lecture at the University, but my husband's a bricklayer, so I suppose we'd count as working-class.' All these, or variants of them, have been reported by the interviewers (students) in informal discussions over the period that the survey has been running. The questions on determinants of class, similarly, ask for 'cultural knowledge' as much as for personal belief, as we argued in Chapter 5: how 'you' describe the middle or the working class depends at least in part on shared definitions of what constitutes these classes. A further problem for interpretation is that it is not clear, on the face of it, that both genders of a given class would be similarly described; it is quite possible that what we are getting from respondents is how they would describe a working-class *man*, and that quite different categories might emerge if we asked how working-class *women* were to be described. This problem, and the problem of tapping knowledge of cultural stereotypes rather than or as well as personal beliefs, is even more acute when we come to analyse the semantic differential questions. Here we have literally no idea whether respondents are picturing a man, a woman, someone known to them, or an average of people they know, or the popular portrayal of (male or female) members of a class in the media, or some sort of sexless and characterless stereotype.

Thirdly, the questionnaire follows existing malestream class research in blindly re-asserting the importance of paid employment in every aspect of people's lives, and in tacitly assuming that all jobs follow the male pattern. There is no indication that people live together in families and thus that the question of 'class' may be ambiguous or have more than one answer depending on whether the self or the household is taken by the respondent as the natural unit of analysis – women being more likely than men to answer in terms of 'household class' because their responsibility for the running of the household makes it perhaps more salient for them than for many men. There is no suggestion that married women's typical financial and structural dependence on their husbands may give them a 'class' which is not fully their own – no attempt to ask what class they might see themselves as belonging to if they were *not* married. The recording of occupational status assumes a male pattern of occupational history – a rising career, or a career plateau, or a steady job. It does not allow for lives in which the type of job is selected with geographical mobility in mind so that the wife can follow the husband in his job moves, or where a career pattern is interrupted by time off to rear children and resumed at a lower level and/or in part-time positions and/or with the hours that may be worked constrained by the end-time of the children's school day. There is no allowance either for a view of life's likely course which suggests that there is no point in making 'career sacrifices' in one's early jobs because precisely this kind of interruption can be foreseen. The People in Society questionnaire was untypical of its period in that it sampled women in their own right and recorded their own current occupation and their own income, but it would have been more useful for this question if it had gone further and recorded first job or highest level achieved or even tried to find a measure of job level which *might* have been achieved if circumstances had been different. These are issues which rarely need to be tackled in research on men, except in such special cases as research on the employment of habitual convicts, but they are the fundamental issues in many women's work lives. It may be that research on men will also have to take them more seriously in the future, if unemployment continues to grow and becomes a 'normal' part of some men's lives. Indeed, it could be argued that the assumptions underlying the use of occupation as a straightforward stratification index are historically and regionally limited even for men. It is only in this century – probably since the Second World War – that permanent, life-long employment has been seen as the norm for men, and then probably only in some regions of the British Isles (see Kumar 1984). Furthermore, even at times and in regions where reasonably full employment obtains, the extent of changes between occupational class over time, by men as well as women, may be far greater and far less patterned than is generally assumed by sociological class theory (see Gilbert 1986).

One further reason why gender differences have not emerged in this book, of course, is that we have not particularly looked for them. To do so would have meant a different and much longer book, and in view of the known limitation of the research instrument it seemed more profitable to concentrate on a descriptive study of *women* in comparable form to what is available on men in the research literature. We may pursue gender comparisons in later papers, however.

Further indication that the wrong questions are being asked or the right ones *not* asked is provided by the difficulty that we and indeed all previous researchers have had in elucidating respondent's overall 'picture' or 'image' of the social world. That women (particularly in the working class) do not appear to make coherent sense of their world does not seem plausible, given the vast amount of psychological and micro-sociological work on the human race as characterized by a 'drive to make sense' and as *perceiving* the world only by means of a body of implicit theory about its nature; yet the results of this and other research would seem to suggest that people's images of class and the social structure are indeed incoherent, made up of propositions which are not mutually congruent. It may be partly that the macrosocial is just not important or salient in most people's lives. At least in part, however, the apparent result would seem to us to be produced by a 'premature closure' on the kinds of questions which are to be asked, the elements out of which a picture of the world must be made up. As we have seen in Chapter 6, most research on images of society has been theory-dominated, hypothesizing 'types' and then trying to find these types among the population, and on the whole the result has been that the types are just not instantiated in sufficient numbers to justify regarding them as of explanatory relevance. The body of theory from which the 'types' have been derived, however, tends to try to explain all of life by the nature of industrial work and/or the experience of living in industrial communities of greater or lesser cohesion. This is a plausible picture of the life of working-class men, though not, we would argue, a correct one; more of life is spent outside the factory than inside it, and that the rest of life has no influence on how one sees the world might be contingently true but can surely not be *assumed* as logically necessary. As a picture of women's lives it is not even plausible; the home is a large part of the life of married women, the industrial work which women perform is often differently organized from that of men because of labour market segmentation and the failure of trade unions to 'grip' the female-dominated industries, and very many women work in jobs which are not industry-related, again for reasons of labour-market segmentation.

The possibility exists, therefore, that there are genuine gender differences in how the social world is perceived, given that women's experience of life is arguably very different from men's. We cannot readily guess what such differences would be and therefore cannot readily frame the questionnaire items which might stand some chance of eliciting them. To try to do so would seem to us a very important endeavour, however, and for two reasons. First, the experience of women and the existence of gender differences seems an important area of research in its own right: the world picture of over half the population can hardly be irrelevant to an understanding of how society is perceived. Secondly, however, it is quite possible that such research might also have very important consequences for our understanding of *men's* social worlds. We have seen that the study of female mobility has important consequences for our understanding of male mobility, and that artefacts are accepted as conclusions if we confine the analysis to males. Even greater consequences might follow, for our understanding of stratification and social structure, from the attempt to articulate gender with class and to build categories which take account of life outside the factory gate and in a country which is no longer dominated (if it ever was) by tight-knit industrial communities. In building a realistic picture of what social life is like for women, we might well find ourselves forced into major revisions of the accepted pictures of what it is like for men. Because one cannot yet tell what the categories would be that proved most useful, however, such research would have to be predominantly ethnographic in character; survey questionnaires can provide answers only to known questions, and the focus of the research in the first instance would have to be on the nature of the questions themselves. A start has been made in this direction with several good ethnographic studies of the lives of (mostly working-class) women, but more is needed.

What we are criticizing here is the essentially reductionist nature of much research on social class, which is cast as though images of society were something separate from the rest of life or confined to some part of life, rather than forming part of the holistic 'theory' through which each person makes sense of his or her world and acts within it. In a longitudinal perspective it is reasonably easy to see that current thinking tends towards reductionism, as we argued in Chapter 4. It is conventional practice, for instance – and we have done it ourselves in this book – to identify 'variables', establish an a priori causal order and go on to argue from correlation to causation. One argues, for instance, that father's class is necessarily the first link in a causal chain, followed by daughter's education (which father's class may influence), followed by the occupational level she is therefore able to achieve, and meanwhile that husband's class is in some way a variable independent of these. We argued in Chapter 4, however, that the causal order of many of these variables is not beyond dispute and that it may vary from woman to woman. For most women, we would agree, educational level partially determines occupational level, but for some it may be true that a decision about the kind of job that she wants to do determines in part whether she stays on at school and what educational qualifications she decides to pursue, so for some educational level, though temporally prior, may in a sense be determined by occupational level. Similarly, the class of the husband she marries is not independent of educational or occupational level. *When* she marries him will certainly not be independent: there are quite marked differences, by occupational class and educational level, in mean age of marriage. *Whom* she marries may also be partly determined, however, because she is more likely to meet and marry one kind of man than another depending on her educational level and the job she pursues. In a sense, therefore, these are not separate 'variables' for some people, but aspects of a single life process, and to talk of one as a causal influence on another is grossly to oversimplify how lives are led.

A similar point may be made cross-sectionally, however, about the nature of *current* life. We are accustomed to speak of 'public sphere' and 'private sphere', for instance – job and politics as opposed to home and children – and to see women as more concerned with the latter than the former, while for men the reverse is the case. (How far it is necessary to strain this argument to assign women's protests over work conditions to the private sphere has already been discussed.) These distinctions are largely ideological artefacts, however; they are not 'how life is', but normative statements of 'how life is to be'. They may sometimes – perhaps often – become internalized in the subjects themselves, so that women themselves feel that their place is with home and children and their men's out at work. This is not a statement of how life is for all women, however (or, for that matter, for all men), and we see no necessity other than a financial one for it to be a statement of how life must be for any women. To import these categories as logically and unanswerably fundamental in research on images of the social world, therefore, is to rest on 'what everyone knows', what is 'taken for granted' – in other words, on the discourse or ideology, not on what actually happens or may sometimes happen or is at least a possibility. Ideological preconceptions are not a sound basis for empirically grounded research.

Finally, the drift of this discussion can be brought into focus by one simple prescription: that questions of theory be separated from problems of technique in the study of women and social class. The theory of class as it is applied to women has been dominated by the technical problem that women's work histories are not like men's and therefore that it is more difficult to assign women than men a class on the basis of their occupations. This purely technical question has tended to dominate the discussion to the extent that it sometimes appears illegitimately to acquire theoretical consequences – that because it is easier to assign class on the basis of husband's job than own job, for instance, that women somehow have no social imagery of their own independent of their husbands'. (Some of the absurdities of this stance were discussed in Chapter 1 and its essential falsity demonstrated in Chapters 4–6.) The questions are distinct, however, and it is our belief that if you assume that women have a class position and a place in society it may sometimes be possible to demonstrate what those positions and those places are. We hope that this book goes some little way towards at least the start of such an endeavour.

References

Abbott, P.A. (1987) Women's Social Class Identification: Does Husband's Occupation Make a Difference? *Sociology* 21: 91–103.

Abbott, P.A. and Sapsford, R.J. (1986) The Class Identification of Married Working Women: a Critical Replication of Ritter and Hargens. *British Journal of Sociology* 38: 535–49.

Abrams, M. (1961) Class and Politics. *Encounter* 17: 39–44.

Abrams, R.H. (1943) Residential Propinquity as a Factor in Marriage Selection. *American Sociological Review* 8: 288–94.

Acker, J.R. (1973) Women and Social Stratification. *American Journal of Sociology* 78: 2–48.

Aitkin, D.A. and Kahan, M. (1974) Australia: Class Politics in the New World. In R. Rose (ed.) *Electoral Politics: A Comparative Yearbook*. New York: Free Press.

Allen, S. (1982) Gender Inequality and Class Formation. In A. Giddens and G. Mackenzie (eds) *Social Class and the Division of Labour*. Cambridge: Cambridge University Press.

Arber, S., Dale, A., and Gilbert, N. (1984) *Evaluating Alternative Measures of Social Class: Does Gender Make a Difference?*. Paper presented to a British Sociological Association Conference, Bradford University.

Arber, S., Dale, A., and Gilbert, N. (1986) The Limitations of Existing Social Class Classifications of Women. In A. Jacoby (ed.) *The Measurement of Social Class: Proceedings of a Conference*. Guildford: Social Research Association.

Athanasiou, R. and Yoshika, G.A. (1973) The Spatial Character of Friendship Formation. *Environment and Behaviour* 5: 288–94.

Attwood, M. and Hatton, F. (1983) Getting On: Gender Differences in Career Development – a Comparative Study in the Hairdressing Industry. In E. Gamarnikow *et al.* (eds) *Gender, Class and Work*. London: Heinemann.

Batstone, E. (1975) Deference and the Ethos of Small Town Capitalism. In M. Bulmer (ed.) *Working Class Images of Society*. London: Routledge Direct Editions.

Beck, S.H. (1983) The Role of Other Family Members in Intergenerational Occupational Mobility. *Sociological Quarterly* 24: 273–85.

Beechey, V. (1984) *Women's Employment in Contemporary Britain*. Paper presented to a British Sociological Association conference, Bradford University.

Blackburn, R.M. and Mann, M. (1975) Ideology in the Non-Skilled Working Class. In M. Bulmer (ed.) *Working Class Images of Society*. London: Routledge Direct Editions.

Blau, P.M. and Duncan, O.D. (1967) *The American Occupational Structure*. New York: Wiley.

Blondel, J. (1965) *Voters, Parties and Leaders*. Harmondsworth, Penguin.

Bose, C. (1973) *Jobs and Gender*. Baltimore: Johns Hopkins University, Center for Metropolitan Planning and Research.

Bossard, J.H.S. (1932) Residential Propinquity as a Factor in Mate Selection. *American Journal of Sociology* 38: 219–24.

Bott, E. (1957) *Family and Social Network*. London: Tavistock.

Bottomore, T.B. (1964) *Elites and Society*. London: Watts.

Braverman, H. (1980) The Transformation of Office Work. In T. Nichols (ed.) *Capital and Labour: Studies in the Capitalist Labour Process*. London: Fontana.

Britten, N. (1984) Class Images in a National Sample of Women and Men. *British Journal of Sociology* 15: 407–34.

Britten, N. and Heath, A. (1983) Women, Men and Social Class. In E. Gamarnikow, D. Morgan, J. Purvis, and D. Taylorson (eds) *Gender, Class and Work*. London: Heinemann.

Bulmer, M. (1975) Some Problems of Research into Class Imagery. In M. Bulmer (ed.) *Working Class Images of Society*. London: Routledge Direct Editions.

Butler, D.E. and King, A. (1965) *The British General Election 1964*. London: Macmillan.

Butler, D.E. and Stokes, D. (1974) *Political Change in Britain: the Evolution of Electoral Choice* 2nd edn. London: Macmillan.

Carter, L. (1974) Agricultural Workers in the Class Structure: a Critical Note. *Sociological Review* 22: 271–79.

Cavendish, R. (1982) *On the Line*. London: Routledge & Kegan Paul.

Chapman, A.D. (1984) Patterns of Mobility among Men and Women in Scotland: 1930–1970. Unpublished Ph.D. thesis, Plymouth Polytechnic.

Chase, I.D. (1975) A Comparison of Men's and Women's Intergenerational Mobility in the United States. *American Sociological Review* 40: 483–505.

Cousins, J. and Brown, R. (1970) Shipbuilding. In J.C. Dewndey (ed.) *Durham County and City with Teeside*. Durham: British Association for the Advancement of Science.

Cousins, J. and Brown, R. (1975) Patterns of Paradox: Shipbuilding

Workers' Images of Society. In M. Bulmer (ed.) *Working Class Images of Society*. London: Routledge Direct Editions.

Coxon, A.P.M. and Jones, C.E. (1978) *The Images of Occupational Prestige: a Study in Social Cognition*. Edinburgh: Macmillan.

Coyle, A. (1984) *Redundant Women*. London: Women's Press.

Crewe, I. (1979) Who Swung Tory? *The Economist* 271 (12 May): 26–7.

Crewe, I. (1983) How Labour was Trounced All Round. *Guardian* 14 June.

Crewe, I., Alt, J., and Fox, T. (1976) Non-Voting in British General Elections 1966–1974. In C. Crouch (ed.) *British Political Sociology Yearbook* 3. London: Croom Helm.

Crompton, R. and Jones, G. (1984) *White Collar Proletariat: Deskilling and Gender in Manual Work*. London: Macmillan.

Crompton, R. and Mann, M. (1986) *Gender and Stratification*. Cambridge: Polity Press.

Curran, J. (1978) Class Imagery, Work Environment and Community: Some Further Findings and a Brief Comment. *British Journal of Sociology* 32: 111–26.

Dahrendorf, R. (1959) *Class and Class Conflict in Industrial Society*. London: Routledge & Kegan Paul.

Dale, A., Gilbert, N., and Arber, S. (1983) *Alternative Approaches to the Measurement of Social Class for Women and Families*. Report to the Equal Opportunities Commision.

Dale, A., Gilbert, G.N., and Arber, S. (1985) Integrating Women into Class Theory. *Sociology* 19: 384–408.

Davis, H. (1979) *Beyond Class Images*. Beckenham: Croom Helm.

Davis, H. and Cousins, J. (1975) The New Working Class and the Old. In M. Bulmer (ed.) *Working Class Images of Society*. London: Routledge Direct Editions.

Delphy, C. (1977) *The Main Enemy*. London: Women's Research and Resources Centre Publications.

Delphy, C. (1981) Women in Stratification Studies. In H. Roberts (ed.) *Doing Feminist Research*. London: Routledge & Kegan Paul.

Delphy, C. (1984) *Close to Home*. London: Hutchinson.

Delphy, C. and Leonard, D. (1986) Class Analysis, Gender Analysis and the Family. In R. Crompton and M. Mann (eds) *Gender and Stratification*. Cambridge: Polity Press.

Dex, S. (1984) *Women's Work Histories*. London: HMSO, DOE Research Paper No. 46.

Dex, S. (1985) *The Sexual Division of Work*. Brighton: Wheatsheaf.

Downs, A. (1957) *An Economic Theory of Democracy*. New York: Harper & Row.

Durant, H. (1966) Voting Behaviour in Britain. In R. Rose (ed.) *Studies in British Politics*. London: Macmillan.

Ebbesen, E.B., Kjos, G.L., and Konecni, V.K. (1976) Spatial Ecology: Its Effects on the Choice of Friends and Enemies. *Journal of Experimental Social Psychology* 12: 508–18.

Eichler, M. (1980) *The Double Standard*. Beckenham: Croom Helm.

England, P. (1979) Women and Occupational Prestige: a Case of Vicarious Sex Equality. *Signs* 4: 252–65.

Erikson, R. (1984) The Social Class of Men, Women and Families. *Sociology* 18: 500–14.

Erikson, R. and Pontinen, S. (1985) Social Mobility in Finland and Sweden: a Comparison of Men and Women. In R. Alapuro *et al.* (eds) *Small States in Comparative Perspective*. Oslo: Norwegian University Press.

Finch, J. (1983) *Married to the Job: Wives' Incorporation in Men's Work*. London: Allen & Unwin.

Fox, A.J. and Goldblatt, P.O. (1982) Socio-Demographic Differences in Mortality. *Population Trends* 27.

Garnsey, E. (1978) Women's Work and Theories of Class Stratification. *Sociology* 12: 223–43.

Giddens, A. (1973) *The Class Structure of the Advanced Societies*. London: Hutchinson.

Gilbert, N. (1985) Occupational Class and Inter-Class Mobility. *British Journal of Sociology* 37: 370–91.

Glass, D.V. (ed.) (1954) *Social Mobility in Britain*. London: Routledge & Kegan Paul.

Glenn, N.D., Ross, A.A., and Tully, J.C. (1974) Patterns of Intergenerational Mobility of Females Through Marriage. *American Sociological Review* 39: 683–99.

Goldthorpe, J.H. (1970) L'Image des classes chez les travailleurs manuels. *Revue Française de Sociologie* 11: 311–38.

Goldthorpe, J.H. (1983) Women and Class Analysis: in Defence of the Conventional View. *Sociology* 17: 465–88.

Goldthorpe, J.H. (1984) Women and Class Analysis: a Reply to the Replies. *Sociology* 18: 491–99.

Goldthorpe, J.H. and Hope, K. (1974) *The Social Grading of Occupations*. Cambridge: Cambridge University Press.

Goldthorpe, J.H., Llewelyn, C. and Payne, C. (1980) *Social Mobility and Class Structure in Modern Britain*. Oxford: Oxford University Press.

Goldthorpe, J.H., Lockwood, D., Bechhofer, F., and Platt, J. (1969) *The Affluent Worker in the Class Structure*. Oxford: Oxford University Press.

Goldthorpe, J.H. and Payne, C. (1986) On the Class Mobility of Women: Results from Different Approaches to the Analysis of Recent British Data. *Sociology* 20: 531–55.

Goot, M. and Reid, E. (1975) *Women and Voting Studies: Mindless Matrons or Sexist Scientism*. Beverley Hills: Sage.

Graetz, B.R. (1983) Images of Class in Modern Society: Structure, Sentiment and Social Location. *Sociology* 17: 77–96.

Greenhalgh, C. and Stewart, M.B. (1982) *Occupational Status and Mobility of Men and Women.* University of Warwick: Warwick Economic Papers No. 211.

GRO (General Register Office) (1966) *Census 1961: England and Wales – Occupational Tables.* London: HMSO.

Haavio-Manilla, E. (1969) Some Consequences of Women's Emancipation. *Journal of Marriage and the Family* 31.

Hakim, C. (1979) *Occupational Segregation.* London: Department of Employment, DOE Research Paper No. 9.

Hall, J. and Jones, D.C. (1950) The Social Grading of Occupation. *British Journal of Sociology* 1: 31–55.

Halsey, A.H. (1978) *Change in British Society.* Oxford: Oxford University Press.

Halsey, A.H., Heath, A., and Ridge, J.M. (1981) *Origins and Destinations: Family, Class and Education in Modern Britain.* Oxford: Oxford University Press.

Harris, A.I. and Clausen, R. (1967) *Labour Mobility in Great Britain 1953–1963.* London: HMSO.

Hartmann, H. (1976) Capitalism, Patriarchy and Job Segregation by Sex. *Signs* 1: 137–69.

Haug, M.R. (1973) Class Measurement and Women's Occupational Roles. *Social Forces* 52: 85–97.

Hauser, R.M., Dickinson, P.J., Travis, H.P., and Koffel, J.M. (1975) Temporal Changes in Occupational Mobility: Evidence for Men in the United States. *American Sociological Review*, 40: 279–97.

Heath, A. (1981) *Social Mobility.* London: Fontana.

Heath, A. and Britten, N. (1984) Women's Jobs do Make a Difference. *Sociology* 18: 475–90.

Heath, A., Jowell, R., and Curtice, J. (1985) *How Britain Votes.* Oxford: Pergamon.

Henry, J. (1979) *Survey Project Guide.* In Open University course DE304 *Research Methods in Education and the Social Sciences.* Milton Keynes: The Open University Press.

Henry, J. (1981) *Survey Project Guide.* In Open University course DE801 *An MSc in Advanced Research Methods.* Milton Keynes: The Open University Press.

Hiller, D.V. and Philliber, W.H. (1982) Derivation of Status Benefits from Occupational Attainments of Married Wives. *Journal of Marriage and the Family* 40: 63–69.

Hiller, P. (1975a) The Nature and Social Location of Everyday Conceptions of Class. *Sociology* 9: 1–28.

Hiller, P. (1975b) Continuities and Variations in Everyday Conceptual

Components of Class. *Sociology* 9: 255–87.

Himmelweit, H., Humphreys, P.C., and Jaeger, M. (1981) *How Voters Decide*. Milton Keynes: The Open University Press.

Himmelweit, S. (1983) *Overcoming Dualism and Transcending Production: a Contribution to the Development of a Marxist-Feminist Methodology*. The Open University, Social Sciences Working Papers.

Hindess, B. (1981) The Politics of Social Mobility. *Economy and Society* 10: 184–202.

Holland, J. (1981) *Work and Women*. Bedford Way Papers No. 6.

Hunt, P. (1980) *Gender and Class Consciousness*. London: Macmillan.

Jackman, M.R. and Jackman, R.W. (1983), *Class Identification in the United States*. Berkeley: University of California Press.

Jackson, B. and Marsden, D. (1966) *Education and the Working Class*. Harmondsworth: Penguin.

Jennings, M.K. and Niemi, R.G. (1974) *The Political Character of Adolescence: The Influence of Families and Schools*. Princeton: Harvard University Press.

Johnstone, T. and Rattanis, A. (1981) Social Mobility Without Class. *Economy and Society* 10.

Jones, G. (1986) *Stratification in Youth*. Paper presented to a British Sociological Association conference, Loughborough University.

Kahan, M., Butler, D., and Stokes, D. (1966) On the Analytical Division of Social Class. *British Journal of Sociology* 17: 122–32.

Katz, A.M. and Hill, R. (1958) Residential Propinquity and Marital Selection: a Review of Theory, Method and Fact. *Marriage and Family Lives* 20: 327–35.

Kelsall, R.K., Kelsall, H.M., and Chisholm, L. (1984) *Stratification* 2nd edn. London: Longman.

Kluegel, J.R., Singleton, T., and Starnes, C.E. (1977) Subjective Class Identification: a Multiple Indicator Approach. *American Sociological Review* 42: 599–611.

Kumar, K. (1984) Unemployment as a Problem in the Development of Industrial Societies: the English Experience. *Sociological Review* 32: 185–233.

Lane, R. (1959) *Political Life*. Glencoe, Illinois: Free Press.

Lansing, M. (1977) *Comparison of the Voting Turnout and Party Choice of British and American Women*. Paper presented to the European Joint Sessions, Berlin.

Lazarsfeld, P.F., Berelson, B., and Gaudet, H. (1968) *The People's Choice* 2nd edn. Chicago: University of Chicago Press.

Lipset, S.M. and Bendix, R. (1959) *Social Mobility in Industrial Society*. London: Heinemann.

Llewellyn, C. (1981) Occupational Mobility and the Use of the Comparative Method. In H. Roberts (ed.) *Doing Feminist Research*.

London: Routledge & Kegan Paul.

Lockwood, D. (1958) *The Black-Coated Worker*. London: Allen & Unwin.

Lockwood, D. (1986) Class, Status and Gender. In R. Crompton and M. Mann (eds) *Gender and Stratification*. Cambridge: Polity Press.

Maccoby, E., Matthews, R., and Morton, A.S. (1954) Youth and Political Change. *Public Opinion Quarterly* 18: 23–9.

MacEwan Scott, A. (1986) Industrialization, Gender Segregation and Stratification Theory. In R. Crompton and M. Mann (eds), *Gender and Stratification*. Cambridge: Polity Press.

McKee, P. (1981) *Statistics of Politics*. In Open University course D291 *Statistical Sources*. Milton Keynes: The Open University Press.

Mackenzie, G. (1975) World Images and the World of Work. In G. Esland *et al.* (eds) *People and Work*. Edinburgh: Holmes McDougall.

Mackenzie, R.T. and Silver, A.I. (1964) Conservatism, Industrialism and the Working Class Tory in England. Louvain: International Sociological Association: *Transactions of the Fifth World Congress of Sociology* 3: 191–202.

McRae, S. (1986) *Cross-Class Families: a Study of Wives' Occupational Superiority*. Oxford: Oxford University Press.

Martin, F.M. (1954) Some Subjective Aspects of Social Stratification, in D.V. Glass *et al.* (eds), *Social Mobility in Britain*. London: Routledge & Kegan Paul.

Martin, J. and Roberts, C. (1984) *Women and Employment: a Lifetime Perspective*. London: HMSO.

Miliband, R. (1969) *The State in Capitalist Society*. London: Weidenfeld & Nicolson.

Millett, K. (1971) *Sexual Politics*. London: Hart-Davis.

Moorhouse, J. (1976) Attitudes to Class and Class Relationships in Britain. *Sociology* 10: 469–96.

Morgan, D.H.J. and Taylorson, D.E. (1983) Class and Work: Bringing Women Back In. In E. Gamarnikow *et al.* (eds) *Gender, Class and Work*. London: Heinemann.

Murgatroyd, L. (1982a) Gender and Class Stratification. Unpublished D.Phil. Thesis, University of Oxford.

Murgatroyd, L. (1982b) Gender and Occupational Stratification. *Sociological Review* 30, 574–602.

Murphy, R. (1984) The Structure of Closure: a Critique and Development of the Theories of Weber, Collins and Parkin. *British Journal of Sociology* 35: 547–67.

Newby, H. (1979) *The Deferential Worker*. Harmondsworth: Penguin.

Nichols, T. (1979) Social Class: Official, Sociological and Marxist. In J. Irvine *et al.* (eds) *Demystifying Social Statistics*. London: Pluto Press.

NOP (National Opinion Polls) (1972) *NOP Bulletin No. 109*. London: National Opinion Polls.

Oakley, A. and Oakley, R. (1979) Sexism in Official Statistics. In J. Irvine *et al.* (eds) *Demystifying Social Statistics*. London: Pluto Press.

OPCS (Office of Population Censuses and Surveys) (1970) *Registrar General's Classification of Occupations*. London: HMSO.

OPCS (1982) *General Household Survey 1980*. London: HMSO.

OPCS (1983a) *Census 1981: Sex, Age and Marital Status – Great Britain*. London: HMSO.

OPCS (1983b) *Census 1981: National Report – Great Britain, Part 2*. London: HMSO.

OPCS (1984) *Census 1981: Economic Activity – Great Britain*. London: HMSO.

OPCS (1985) *General Household Survey 1985*. London: HMSO.

Osborne, A.F. and Morris, T.C. (1979) The Rationale for a Composite Index of Social Class and its Evaluation. *British Journal of Sociology* 30: 39–60.

Ossowski, S. (1963) *Class Structure in the Social Consciousness*. London: Routledge & Kegan Paul.

Pahl, J. (1980) Patterns of Money Management within Marriage. *Journal of Social Policy* 9: 313–35.

Pahl, J. (1983) The Allocation of Money and the Structuring of Inequality within Marriage. *Sociological Review* 31: 237–62.

Pahl, R. (1985) *Divisions of Labour*. Oxford: Blackwell.

Pahl, R. and Wallace, C. (1985) Household Work Strategies in Economic Recession. In E. Mingione and N. Redclift (eds) *Beyond Employment*. Oxford: Blackwell.

Parkin, F. (1972) *Class Inequality and the Political Order: Social Stratification in Capitalist and Communist Countries*. St Albans: Paladin.

Parkin, F. (1979) *Marxism and Class Theory: a Bourgeois Critique*. London: Tavistock.

Phillips, A. and Taylor, B. (1980) Sex and Skill: Notes Towards a Feminist Analysis. *Feminist Review* 6: 79–88.

Platt, J. (1971) Variations in Answers to Different Questions of Perceptions of Class. *Sociological Review* 19: 31–2.

Plowman, D.E.G., Minchington, W.E., and Stacey, M. (1962) Local Social Status in England and Wales. *Sociological Review* 10: 161–82.

Porter, M. (1983) *Home, Work and Class Consciousness*. Manchester: Manchester University Press.

Poulantzas, N. (1975) *Classes in Contemporary Capitalism*. London: New Left Books.

Prandy, K. (1986) Similarities of Life-Style and Occupations of Women. In R. Crompton and M. Mann (eds) *Gender and Stratification*. Cambridge: Polity Press.

Randall, V. (1982) *Women and Politics*. London: Macmillan.

Reid, I. (1977) Your Chance to Have a Say. *Homes and Gardens* 4: 79–84.

204 *Women and Social Class*

Reid, I. (1980) *Social Class Differences in Britain*. London: Grant McIntyre.

Ritter, K.V. and Hargens, L.L. (1975) Occupational Positions and Class Identification of Married Working Women: a Test of the Asymmetry Hypothesis. *American Journal of Sociology*. 80: 934–48.

Roberts, H. (1985) Women and Social Class. *Survey Methods Newsletter*, Spring: 3–4.

Roberts, H. (1986) *The Social Classification of Women: a Life-Cycle Approach*. Paper presented to a British Sociological Association conference, Loughborough University.

Roberts, H. (1987) *Women and Social Classification*. Brighton: Wheatsheaf.

Roberts, K., Cook, F.G., Clark, S.C. and Semeonoff, E. (1977) *The Fragmentary Class Structure*. London: Heinemann.

Rose, R. (1976) Social Structure and Party Differences. In R. Rose (ed.) *Studies in British Politics*. London: Macmillan.

Rosenfeld, R.A. (1978) Women's Intergenerational Occupational Mobility. *American Sociological Review* 48: 36–46.

Runciman, W.G. (1964) Embourgeoisement, Self-Rated Class and Party Preference. *Sociological Review* 12: 137–54.

Runciman, W.G. (1966) *Relative Deprivation and Social Justice*. London: Routledge & Kegan Paul.

Samuel, R. (1960) The Deference Voter. *New Left Review* 1: 9–13.

Seagoe, M.V. (1933) Factors Influencing Selection of Associates. *Journal of Educational Research*. 27: 32–40.

Siltanen, J. and Stanworth, M. (1984) *Women and the Public Sphere: a Critique of Sociology and Politics*. London: Hutchinson.

Smith, D.E. (1979) A Sociology for Women. In J.A. Sherman and E.T. Beck (eds) *The Prism of Sex: Essays in the Sociology of Knowledge*. Wisconsin: University of Wisconsin Press.

Smith, D.E. (1983) Women, Class and Family. In R. Miliband and J. Saville (eds) *The Socialist Register*. London: Merlin.

Stacey, M. (1960) *Tradition and Change: a Study of Banbury*. Oxford: Oxford University Press.

Stanworth, M. (1984) Women and Social Class Analysis: a Reply to Goldthorpe. *Sociology* 18: 159–70.

Taylor, P.J. and Johnstone, R.J. (1979) *The Geography of Elections*. Harmondsworth: Penguin.

Townsend, P. (1979) *Poverty in the United Kingdom: a Study of Household Resources and Standards of Living*. Harmondsworth: Penguin.

Treiman, D.J. (1977) *Occupational Prestige in Comparative Perspective*. New York: Academic Press.

Treiman, D.J. and Terrell, K. (1975) Sex and the Process of Status Attainment: a Comparison of Working Men and Women. *American Sociological Review* 40: 174–200.

Tyre, A. and Treas, J. (1974) The Occupational and Marital Mobility of Women. *American Sociological Review* 39: 293–302.

Vanneman, R. and Pampel, F.C. (1977) The American Perception of Class and Status. *American Sociological Review* 42: 422–37.

Van Velso, E. and Beeghley, L. (1979) The Process of Class Identification among Employed Married Women. *Journal of Marriage and the Family* 41: 771–91.

Walby, S. (1986) Gender, Class and Stratification: Towards a New Approach. In R. Crompton and M. Mann (eds) *Gender and Stratification*. Cambridge: Polity Press.

Webb, S. (1985) *Counter Arguments: an Ethnographic Look at Women and Class*. University of Manchester, Department of Sociology: Studies in Sexual Politics.

Weiner, T.S. (1978) Homogeneity of Political Party Preferences between Spouses. *Journal of Politics* 40: 208–11.

West, J. (1978) Women, Sex and Class. In A. Kuhn and A. Wolpe (eds) *Feminism and Materialism: Women and Modes of Production*. London: Routledge & Kegan Paul.

Westergaard, J.R. (1972) The Myth of Classlessness. In R. Blackburn (ed.) *Ideology in Social Science: Readings in Critical Social Theory*. London: Fontana.

Westergaard, J.R. (1975) Radical Class Consciousness: a Comment. In M. Bulmer (ed.) *Working Class Images of Society*. London: Routledge & Kegan Paul.

Westergaard, J.R. and Little, A. (1967) Educational Opportunity and Social Selection in England and Wales: Trends and Implications. In *Social Objectives in Educational Planning*. Paris: OECD.

Westergaard, J.R. and Resler, H. (1975) *Class in a Capitalist Society: a Study of Contemporary Britain*. London: Heinemann.

Westwood, S. (1984) *All Day Every Day: Factory and Family in the Making of Women's Lives*. London: Pluto Press.

Willener, A. (1957) *Images de la sociéte' et classes sociales*. Berne: Imprimerie Staempfli.

Wright, E.O. (1985) *Classes*. London: Verso.

Young, M. (1952) Distribution of Income within the Family. *British Journal of Sociology* 3: 305–21.

Young, M. and Willmott, P. (1956) Social Grading by Manual Workers. *British Journal of Sociology* 7: 337–45.

Zaretsky, E.V. (1976). *Capitalism, Family and Personal Life*. London: Pluto Press.

Author index

Subject index